This book brings together the combined experience of two senior family law practitioners and fellow members of The Working Group on Pets in Divorce and Separation. The authors' combined experience informs a guide that aims not only to explain the law as it stands, but to support practitioners in navigating one of the most emotionally complex and evolving areas of modern family law.

Sadie Glover

Sadie Glover is a Partner and the Head of Family & Divorce at Blaser Mills Law in Marlow. She is an experienced family law solicitor with over two decades of practice in private family law. Sadie is a recommended lawyer in Legal 500 guide, where she has been noted as being a "titan" and a formidable force".

Alongside her legal work, Sadie is an all-issues Family Mediator, a twice published author (*A Practical Guide to Short Marriages for Family Lawyers, first edition* and the *second edition* which she co-authored with Philip Perrins and Beth Hibbert of 1GC Family Law) and the Co-Chair of the Buckinghamshire and Berkshire Resolution Committee.

Sadie regularly presents for MBL, the leading CPD provider in England and Wales. She is also regularly asked to speak at national family law conferences.

Sadie is the founder of "*Family Law Friends*", the podcast which focusses on wellbeing and connection with the family law community, which she co-hosts with Estella Newbold-Brown.

Estella Newbold-Brown

Estella Newbold-Brown is a Partner and Head of Family Law at Lester Aldridge, based in London. Ranked in both the Legal 500 and Chambers & Partners, she has been described as a "Powerhouse" and a lawyer with so much "energy and drive". Estella specialises in all aspects of private family law and is ranked by Citywealth as a Top 75 Family Lawyer.

Estella regularly speaks at conferences, delivers webinars and appears on podcasts and television discussing the topic of pets and the law. She is the co-founder of the Working Group on Pets on Divorce and Separation, together with barrister, Sarah-Lucy Cooper.

Estella is a member of the London Resolution Committee and is a Resolution accredited specialist. In her spare time, Estella is a children's author, one of her books (Isla and Quinn – The sunflowers) is aimed towards family lawyers to provide as a resource for their clients and for parents who are separating to read to their children.

A shared perspective

Although Sadie Glover and Estella Newbold-Brown bring different professional experiences to this work, they share a common perspective on family law practice. Both recognise the limits of the current legal framework in relation to pets on divorce, and the significant role played by practitioners in managing those limits through advice, negotiation and dispute resolution. This book reflects that shared approach. It is written for family lawyers, by family lawyers, and is rooted in the realities of practice.

A Practical Guide to Pets on Divorce for Family Lawyers

A Practical Guide to Pets on Divorce for Family Lawyers

Sadie Glover LLB Hons

Partner, Mediator & Head of Family Law at Blaser Mills Law

Estella Newbold-Brown LLB

Partner & Head of Family, Lester Aldridge

Law Brief Publishing

The information in this book was believed to be correct at the time of writing. All content is for information purposes only and is not intended as legal advice. No liability is accepted by either the publisher or author for any errors or omissions (whether negligent or not) that it may contain. Professional advice should always be obtained before applying any information to particular circumstances.

Published 2026 by Law Brief Publishing, an imprint of Law Brief Publishing Ltd
30 The Parks
Minehead
Somerset
TA24 8BT

www.lawbriefpublishing.com

Paperback: 978-1-918241-28-0

FOREWORD BY SIR NICHOLAS MOSTYN

Last April my wife and I lost to a rare adrenal cancer our beloved 12 ½ year old miniature dachshund, Bilbo. To say that we were distraught would be an understatement. Only now, nearly a year later, are we able to contemplate acquiring a replacement. Bilbo was far more than a mere chattel. It is interesting that in French there is no direct translation of the word pet. In France Bilbo was *notre animal de compagnie.* And he was thus described on his French passport. That description emphasised his autonomy as a fellow creature, who accompanied us, rather than as a mere item of ownership.

This status of a companion animal is at the heart of this excellent work. The authors say that "in the context of divorce proceedings, pets are treated no differently than a piece of furniture"; and that "the court has no inherent jurisdiction to make orders based on an animal's welfare or best interests". This may be correct as a matter of strict law as applied by conservative and unimaginative judges. Notoriously, as a judge I often had difficulty in discerning the dividing line between what the law is and what it should be. I therefore rail against the notion that a sentient being like a dog is to be treated in a divorce in the same way as a grandfather clock. I would argue that the difference is already recognised in the general law.

The Animal Welfare Act 2006 provides for numerous offences for cruelty to animals as well as for comprehensive registration systems to deal with health and ownership. Now it might be said that the latter aspect does no more than to gives a dog the same status as a motor car; but there is no offence of cruelty to motor cars.

Moreover, Parliament has recognised the unique sentient status of animals in the Animal Welfare (Sentience) Act 2022, which remains sadly unimplemented. When it is brought into effect - and I hope that will be soon - It will require government to have regard to the views of an animal welfare sentience committee whenever it formulates any policy which may impact on the welfare of animals.

With this strong emphasis on the welfare of our fellow creatures in the general law, I cannot see why within the existing discretionary framework for the resolution of financial and property disputes between divorcing spouses, it is not permissible to give have regard, as one of the circumstances of the case, to the best interests of a companion animal, and to make an appropriate property adjustment order, subject to conditions, to give effect to that consideration. This excellent work debates the feasibility of such an approach. It may be that, were a test case to be sent to High Court judge level, the court would not be brave enough to adopt that approach. In my opinion that would be highly regrettable as the prospect of legislation the lines of that in Canada and Australia (which is fully described in the work) looks extremely remote.

In my opinion this is a really important work which should be read by everybody practising financial remedy law.

Sir Nicholas Mostyn

PREFACE

A Practical Guide to Pets on Divorce for Family Lawyers offers family law practitioners a clear, practical guide to one of the fastest-growing and most emotionally charged issues in modern family practice: what happens to the family pet when a relationship breaks down. As pets are increasingly regarded as family members rather than mere property, disputes about their future care, ownership and welfare are becoming more common, and more complex.

In addition to examining the current domestic legal position, the book looks at emerging developments internationally and the growing recognition of pets within family justice systems abroad. These comparative perspectives provide valuable context for practitioners seeking to make creative and persuasive arguments on behalf of their clients.

This book provides practitioners with the legal framework, strategic guidance and practical tools needed to navigate these cases effectively and sensitively.

Our thanks go to our respective firms, Blaser Mills Law and Lester Aldridge. We are so grateful for all your support. Thanks also to Sir Nicholas Mostyn for his foreword, and of course, The Working Group for Pets on Divorce & Separation.

The law stated within this text is correct as of 10 March 2026.

Sadie Glover
Estella Newbold-Brown
March 2026

CONTENTS

Chapter One	Introduction: Pets, Families and the Law	1
Chapter Two	The Legal Status of Pets in England and Wales	5
Chapter Three	The Court's Approach to Pet Disputes	13
Chapter Four	Relevant Case Law on Pets and Divorce	21
Chapter Five	Property Adjustment Orders	37
Chapter Six	Managing Client Expectations	47
Chapter Seven	Non-Court Dispute Resolution in Pet Disputes	53
Chapter Eight	Pet Nups	67
Chapter Nine	Comparative and International Perspectives	71
Chapter Ten	The Working Group on Pets on Divorce & Separation	87
Chapter Eleven	Potential Reform to the Law in England and Wales	95
Chapter Twelve	What Does All of This Mean for Family Practitioners?	99
Chapter Thirteen	Conclusion	103

CHAPTER ONE

PETS, FAMILY AND THE LAW

1.1 Pets now occupy a central and deeply personal place in modern family life. For many people across England and Wales, dogs, cats, and other companion animals are far more than possessions: they are emotional anchors, protectors, and members of the family. The rise of pet ownership in the United Kingdom reflects profound social and demographic changes. More people now live alone, families are formed later in life, cohabitation has increased, and social isolation has become a topic of national concern. In this context, companion animals offer not merely affection, but routine, structure, emotional regulation, and a sense of belonging.

1.2 These benefits become especially salient during relationship breakdown. Family lawyers are very familiar with the reality that, when a marriage or partnership ends, the parties' attachment to their pets often intensifies. Clients frequently describe their dogs or cats as "part of the family", or even as their "child", reflecting not only deep emotional investment but also the day-to-day realities of care, responsibility, and shared domestic life. Pets witness the rhythms of a relationship; they are present during celebrations, losses, and the ordinary routines that form the backdrop to family life. When separation occurs, losing a pet, or losing contact with one, can feel as devastating as the end of the relationship itself.

1.3 Yet English law stands in stark contrast to this emotional and social reality. Under current legislation, pets are classified as chattels: objects to be owned, bought, sold, or transferred exactly like any other form of personal property. In the context of divorce proceedings, this means pets are treated no differently than a piece of furniture. This disconnect between the lived experience of families and the structure of the law in England and Wales can cause genuine shock to clients. Individuals who have acted as a pet's primary carer, by walking, feeding, training, and providing emotional comfort, are often surprised to learn that none of this carries determinative legal weight. Instead, ownership is largely a question of evidence: receipts, microchip registrations, insurance documents, and veterinary records.

1.4 This legal framework produces several difficulties. First, it can feel unfair. The person who has poured time, labour, and emotional energy into an animal may find themselves legally powerless if the other party is the registered owner or can demonstrate legal purchase. Second, it can escalate conflict. Clients who might otherwise resolve financial matters constructively may become entrenched over disputes concerning a beloved pet. Third, it creates practical problems. Courts are reluctant to make detailed orders about ongoing arrangements for pets, and shared-care orders are almost never made, both because of enforcement difficulties and because there is no statutory framework for such arrangements.

1.5 Family practitioners therefore face the delicate task of navigating a legal landscape that has not kept pace with social development. Cases concerning pets are rarely reported, both because they often settle and because judges are keen to avoid establishing broad principles in matters perceived as low financial value. But the emotional value of such disputes is often extremely high. Many solicitors report that pet disputes can be extremely difficult to settle.

1.6 Internationally, the position is evolving. Several jurisdictions have moved away from a strict property approach, incorporating welfare-based considerations or even statutory recognition of animals as sentient beings. These developments highlight the growing recognition that companion animals occupy a unique status, somewhere between property and family members. In England and Wales, however, reform has been slow. Although animal welfare law recognises sentience in other contexts, family law has yet to adopt a framework capable of balancing ownership with welfare considerations.

1.7 This book examines the current law in England and Wales, analyses practical challenges, explores comparative models, and considers pathways for proportionate reform. It aims to equip practitioners with clear guidance while also contributing to a broader conversation about the future of pet-related disputes in family justice.

CHAPTER TWO

THE LEGAL STATUS OF PETS IN ENGLAND AND WALES

2.1 To understand how courts resolve disputes about pets on divorce, one must begin with the basic legal premise: pets are property. While clients often assume there must be a welfare-based framework, or at least flexibility akin to decisions concerning children, nothing of the sort currently exists.

2.2 The current legal view of animals is rooted in centuries-old principles of property law. Historically, animals were valued according to their utility: livestock for food or agricultural work, horses for labour or transport, and dogs for hunting or guarding. Companion animals existed, of course, but their legal status was not derived from emotional attachment. Instead, they were categorised as "goods" or "chattels", forming part of a person's personal property.

2.3 This classification persists today. In legal terms, a dog is not a member of the family but a tangible item, albeit one with unique characteristics. This means that ownership and not welfare, is the central concern. When a couple divorces, the relevant statutory framework is the Matrimonial Causes Act 1973, particularly *section 24*, which empowers the court to make property adjustment orders. These include the transfer of any property, land, money, investments, or chattels from one spouse to another. A pet, therefore, is something that can be transferred under this provision.

2.4 Crucially, the court has no inherent jurisdiction to make orders based on an animal's welfare or "best interests". The welfare principle in *section 1 of the Children Act 1989* applies exclusively to children. Judges cannot extend it to animals, even if both parties feel passionately that welfare considerations should guide the outcome.

2.5 This strict reliance on ownership creates several practical problems. First, ownership may not reflect reality. A dog might be registered in one person's name because they arranged the microchip or paid the adoption fee, even though the other partner performed most of the day-to-day care. Second, documentation may be inconsistent or ambiguous. Microchip registration, for example, is not definitive proof of ownership; it establishes who is responsible for updating details, not necessarily who owns the animal. Courts therefore must weigh a mosaic of evidence, including purchase receipts, registration documents, veterinary records, and behavioural patterns.

2.6 Moreover, English law does not recognise the concept of "shared care" for pets. While couples often share responsibilities during their relationship, shared legal ownership must be consciously established, typically through joint purchase or explicit agreement. In many relationships, couples simply do not consider these questions at the point of acquiring a pet. As a result, shared ownership is often difficult to prove.

2.7 Another complication is that courts prioritise a clean break in financial remedy proceedings. Judicial reluctance to impose ongoing shared arrangements is well-established. Courts avoid crafting orders requiring continuing cooperation between former partners unless absolutely necessary. This principle, combined with the classification of pets as property, means shared-care orders for pets are almost never made. Even if parties request such arrangements, courts tend to discourage them, directing couples instead towards negotiated or informal agreements.

2.8 Client expectations can therefore be at odds with legal reality. A person who views their pet as a family member may feel bewildered to discover that the law treats disputes in a manner akin to determining ownership of a household object. For practitioners, managing these expectations is an essential early task. A clear explanation of the legal framework is often necessary to reduce shock, disappointment, or escalating conflict.

2.9 Despite these constraints, there is some flexibility. The court can consider practical factors indirectly, such as who is better placed to house the pet or who has more stable working hours, but these points serve only to highlight ownership, they do not form an independent welfare test. For example, if evidence of ownership is evenly balanced, judges may take into account who has historically provided day-to-day care or who has a stronger emotional relationship with the animal. But such considerations are not determinative; they merely guide interpretation of the underlying property question.

2.10 Looking forward, the persistence of this strict property approach raises important questions about whether the law remains fit for purpose. Society increasingly views pets as family members, and the emotional stakes in pet disputes can be exceptionally high. Yet the law offers only a narrow conceptual lens through which to resolve them. This tension forms the foundation for later chapters assessing comparative reform and the work of the Working Group on Pets on Divorce & Separation, of which the authors are members.

2.11 It should be noted that this is not a book about animals, generally. It is however appropriate to refer to certain aspects of the law, for the sake of completeness.

2.12 Although the formal legal status of a domesticated animal is that of a chattel, the law recognises that such creatures have attributes which are far more extensive than those possessed by non-sentient objects. Therefore, Halsbury's Laws has nearly half a volume on the law relating to animals, covering such things as:

- the health of animals;

- the welfare of animals and the protection of animals from cruelty, including the regulation of scientific experiments on animals;

- the keeping of animals in establishments such as zoos or riding stables;

- the keeping, breeding and sale of dogs. Including dangerous dogs;

- certain criminal and civil liabilities of owners or keepers for damage caused by their animals

2.13 All of these aspects are governed by primary or secondary legislation. In contrast Halsbury's Laws states that "*the principles of ownership of animals are derived from the common law, which has been long settled*".

It says:

> "*Domestic animals, like other personal and movable chattels, are the subject of absolute property. The owner can maintain a claim for their detention or conversion, or for trespass to goods in respect of them, and retains property in them if they stray or are lost*"

2.14 That said, there is obviously a considerable difference between an inanimate object and a sentient being. For this reason there are many legal rules relating to animals that simply do not apply to inanimate objects. For example, there are rules relating to the registration of ownership. All horses, donkeys and ponies must be microchipped and the details recorded in a passport.

2.15 In the UK, there are currently 81 Passport Issuing Organisations (PIOs). While the BHS is one of the most common for "ID-only" passports, most PIOs are specialized Breed Societies that manage specific studbooks. All individual PIO records (including the BHS's) feed into the UK Central Equine Database. This is the only national register. An owner can use the National Chipchecker to see if a horse's microchip is correctly registered to them in the national database.

It is not possible to change ownership directly on the CED; it must be done through the horse's specific passport issuer (like the BHS), who then updates the CED automatically.

Regardless of which organization issued the passport, the following rules are strictly enforced as of March 2026:

The "30-Day" Rule: When you buy a horse, you have exactly 30 days to send the passport to the relevant PIO to update the ownership.

You must return the passport to the issuing PIO within 30 days of a horse's death to have it invalidated.

Although the name of the last recorded owner in the passport is not conclusive, it will be very powerful evidence of ownership.

Dogs

2.16 Microchipping has been compulsory for all dogs in England, Scotland, Wales, and Northern Ireland since 2016. Puppies must be microchipped and registered by the time they are 8 weeks old. The breeder is legally responsible for microchipping them and registering themselves as the first owner before the puppy leaves for its new home. If you are buying a puppy, you must keep your contact details (phone, address) up to date on the database. Failure to do so is a secondary offence, with a fine of up to £500.

Cats (England Only)

2.17 A major legal change occurred in 2024, making microchipping mandatory for pet cats in England. All pet cats must be microchipped by the time they reach 20 weeks of age. There is no exemption for indoor-only cats. They must be chipped because they can still escape or be stolen. If your cat is found without a chip, you will be given 21 days to comply. If you don't, you can be fined up to £500.

Vaccination record

2.18 An up-to-date vaccination card is an almost legal requirement for cats and dogs. As with horses, the name of the owner on an animal health certificate for travel abroad or on the vaccination card or on the microchip register will be extremely strong proof of ownership.

Liability for injury caused by your animal.

2.19 Animals Act 1971. This sought to put extremely convoluted common law rules on a statutory footing but as a decision of the House of Lords in *Mirvahedy v Henley [2003] UKHL 16,* showed the new law was scarcely less torturous. This case is famous (and somewhat controversial) because it established that a keeper can be held strictly liable for damage or injury caused by an animal, even if the owner was not negligent and the animal was behaving "normally" for its species in those specific circumstances. Note that the strict liability applies to the owner or keeper of an animal.

Offences of cruelty to animals

2.20 The Animal Welfare Act 2006 creates a number of offences in relation to its aims of the prevention of harm to animals and the promotion of the welfare of animals, upon conviction of which the offender is liable to a fine or imprisonment or both; and in addition orders may be made for deprivation of ownership, disqualification from owning or keeping animals, the seizure or destruction of animals, the forfeiture of equipment used in offences, and the cancellation of, or disqualification from holding, a licence. Extensive powers of inspection, search and seizure are conferred by the Act in relation to animals in distress, animal fights and other offences; in relation to licences and registration; for the inspection of farm premises; and to ensure compliance with EU obligations.

2.21 The Animal Welfare Act 2006 also provides for the registration and licensing of activities involving animals, for the issue of codes of practice to provide practical guidance in respect of any provision made by or under the Act, and for the appointment of inspectors.

2.22 These extensive rules recognise that an animal is a sentient being. The **Animal Welfare (Sentience) Act 2022** provides that the Animal Sentience Committee will be established by the Secretary of State as from a day to be appointed. The purpose of the Act is stated to be: "*An Act to make provision for an Animal Sentience Committee with functions relating to the effect of government policy on the welfare of animals as sentient beings.*"

2.23 When any government policy is being or has been formulated or implemented, the Animal Sentience Committee may make recommendations for the purpose of ensuring that, in any further formulation or implementation of the policy, the government has all due regard to the ways in which the policy might have an adverse effect on the welfare of animals as sentient beings. Unfortunately, this Act is yet to come into force.

Conclusion

2.24 It is fair to say that the object of the 2006 and 2022 Acts is to promote the welfare of animals as sentient beings. Where there is a dispute in divorce proceedings between two persons over the care and control of a pet, it is therefore not a big reach for the court, in its consideration of all the circumstances of the case, to promote the welfare of the animal as a sentient being.

2.25 Technically there is no impediment to giving effect to a welfare-based decision. The ownership of the animal by the party who is given its care and control can be achieved by a property adjustment order (if that party is not already the owner).

CHAPTER THREE

THE COURT'S APPROACH TO PET DISPUTES

3.1 Disputes involving pets on divorce sit at the intersection of strong emotion and a legal framework that offers very little flexibility. Although clients frequently approach these disputes assuming the court will consider factors such as who has the closer bond with the animal or who has provided the bulk of day-to-day care, the judiciary is constrained by the classification of pets as chattels and by the need for procedural proportionality. As a result, the court's approach remains limited, pragmatic and ownership-focused, even where the parties' positions are driven by deeply personal attachment.

3.2 This chapter explores in detail how the Court actually determines pet disputes, the evidential considerations that arise, the judicial reasoning that underpins these decisions, and the procedural pressures that influence how cases are managed. It also addresses the significant gap between client expectation and legal reality, a recurring theme for practitioners who handle disputes involving pets.

Ownership

3.3 The most important principle governing the court's approach is that ownership is the central and often decisive question. The court does not start from the premise of fairness, emotional attachment or welfare. Instead, judges treat pets as items of personal property whose ownership must be established using conventional principles. This means that in almost every case concerning a dog, cat or other companion animal, the court begins by asking the same question it would ask about a vehicle or an artwork: "*Who owns this property*"?

3.4 Ownership may arise through purchase, gift, joint acquisition, or sometimes through inferred transfer. But in all cases, it is ownership, not care, affection or responsibility, that guides judicial decision-making. This starting point can feel harsh to clients. Many separating couples have formed deep emotional connections with their animals. Nevertheless, the courts must apply the law as it stands, which currently offers no basis for elevating welfare or attachment above ownership.

How ownership is established

3.5 The courts rely on a combination of documentary and behavioural evidence to determine ownership. Because disputes often arise years after a pet is acquired, evidence may be incomplete or conflicting, requiring the court to piece together a coherent narrative from imperfect records and the parties' recollections.

Purchase documentation

3.6 Purchase receipts, adoption agreements or breeder contracts are often the strongest indicators of ownership. If only one party signed the agreement or paid the upfront cost, this can be highly persuasive, although not determinative. If an animal was adopted from a rescue organisation, the adoption paperwork typically names the adopter; courts often give this considerable weight.

Microchip registration

3.7 Microchip details form part of the evidential mosaic, but they do not conclusively establish ownership. Registration identifies the person responsible for updating information, it does not operate as a title register. Confusion arises because many clients believe that microchip records function like a land registry for pets; practitioners must explain that while helpful, such evidence is not definitive.

Veterinary and insurance records

3.8 Veterinary registration forms, vaccination certificates and insurance policies are also examined. These often reflect the person who deals with administrative tasks rather than the person who undertakes daily care. Courts consider these records alongside broader evidence, but again, they are not treated as absolute proof.

Financial contributions

3.9 Regular payment for food, insurance, grooming, training, or other costs can indicate responsibility and involvement, though it rarely establishes legal ownership on its own. In many relationships, one partner pays routine bills while the other assumes greater caregiving responsibilities.

Day-to-day care

3.10 Evidence about who walks, feeds, trains and generally cares for the animal is relevant but not determinative. Courts may use this evidence to support or undermine assertions of ownership, but day-to-day care alone seldom translates into legal ownership. This is one of the most difficult messages for practitioners to deliver to clients.

Behavioural evidence and the pet's preference

3.11 Unlike some international jurisdictions that consider an animal's welfare or "best interests", English courts do not factor a pet's preference into their decisions. Behavioural evidence, for example, that a dog appears more bonded to one party, may be emotionally compelling but is rarely relevant in law.

Intention of the parties

3.12 Where documentation is unclear or ownership is genuinely shared, courts may look at the parties' intentions when acquiring the animal. Did both parties intend shared ownership? Was the pet acquired for one individual (e.g., as a birthday gift), or was it understood to belong to one person?

Gifts, joint ownership and transfers during the relationship

3.13 Clients frequently rely on arguments that a pet was gifted to them or that ownership transferred during the relationship. Courts therefore pay close attention to the law of gifts. To establish a valid gift, the receiving party must prove:

1. Intention to give,
2. Delivery of the item, and
3. Acceptance by the recipient.

3.14 Pet-related gifts can be ambiguous. A partner might say, "*I got this dog for you*" in an affectionate sense without intending to relinquish legal ownership. Courts are cautious in these situations, examining context, behaviour, and documentary evidence to determine genuine intention.

3.15 Joint ownership presents similar difficulties. Many couples jointly care for pets without formalising ownership. To prove joint ownership, a party must provide evidence of joint contribution, joint intention, or conduct from which joint ownership can properly be inferred. In practice, this threshold can be hard to meet.

Judicial reluctance to order shared care

3.16 One of the most striking features of English case law on pets is judicial reluctance to impose ongoing shared-care arrangements. While shared care might appear to offer fairness or reflect pre-separation routines, courts routinely decline to make such orders for several reasons:

3.17 There is no enabling framework for pet-sharing orders equivalent to the Children Act 1989. Without statutory authority, courts are hesitant to craft bespoke, ongoing arrangements.

3.18 Shared care requires cooperation between former partners. Courts aim to deliver finality in financial remedy proceedings and avoid orders requiring continuous post-divorce involvement. A shared-care order for a pet is likely to generate disputes about timing, handover, emergencies, holidays and costs, problems the court has neither the resources nor procedural tools to manage.

3.19 Judges consistently emphasise proportionality when allocating judicial time. Crafting a detailed arrangement for a pet can be seen as disproportionate, especially where the parties' financial disputes remain unresolved.

3.20 Courts are alert to the risk that, far from resolving matters, shared-care orders may exacerbate conflict. A pet, unwittingly, may become a proxy for emotional grievances arising from the relationship breakdown.

3.21 For these reasons, although private agreements or side letters can include shared-care arrangements, courts almost never order them.

Disputes involving multiple pets

3.22 Cases involving more than one pet introduce additional complexity. In some circumstances, courts have separated pets between parties to avoid joint ownership. This can be deeply distressing for clients, particularly where animals are bonded siblings. Yet the court's role is confined to resolving legal ownership, not managing animal welfare.

3.23 When ownership is unclear, courts may allocate different pets to each party on pragmatic grounds, especially where doing so resolves the dispute quickly and avoids ongoing entanglement.

Proportionality and the Court's case management powers

3.24 Judges frequently emphasise that financial remedy proceedings should not be dominated by disputes involving low-value chattels. While the emotional stakes may be high, courts must manage their lists efficiently, resolve cases within reasonable timeframes, and ensure proportionality. As a result:

- Judges may refuse to list a separate hearing solely for a pet dispute.
- Parties may be encouraged, or directed, to resolve the issue through negotiation, mediation or arbitration.
- The issue may be addressed as part of broader financial proceedings rather than in isolation.

3.25 Courts are well aware that disproportionate litigation drains resources, increases conflict, and rarely yields satisfactory outcomes.

Private agreements

3.26 Given the limitations of the court's powers, judges routinely encourage parties to reach private agreements about pets. These may take the form of:

- informal agreements,
- side letters between solicitors,
- arbitration decisions, or
- mediated outcomes.

3.27 Courts prefer such arrangements because they allow parties to adopt welfare-based approaches that judges themselves cannot. Parties are free to agree shared care, joint responsibility, or any arrangement that reflects their circumstances and the pet's needs.

Client expectations versus the legal position

3.28 Perhaps the most enduring challenge for practitioners is managing client expectations. Many clients enter discussions believing that:

- the court will consider the pet's welfare,
- emotional attachment will carry legal weight,
- a shared-care arrangement is likely, or
- the court can impose contact.

None of these assumptions align with current law.

3.29 The professional task, therefore, is to guide clients sensitively, ensuring they understand the legal limitations without diminishing their emotional experience. Clear early advice can help clients shift towards constructive negotiation and non-court resolution, avoiding costly, distressing and ultimately unsuccessful litigation.

CHAPTER FOUR

RELEVANT CASE LAW ON PETS AND DIVORCE

4.1 Case law concerning pets in the context of divorce and financial remedy proceedings is sparse but highly instructive. The limited number of published decisions reflects a combination of factors: judicial reluctance to devote substantial court time to low-value chattel disputes, parties' desire for privacy, the tendency for such issues to settle, and the lack of a statutory welfare framework for companion animals. Yet the cases that *have* reached judgment, whether reported or discussed in professional commentary, illustrate the judiciary's consistent adherence to property principles and provide useful guidance for practitioners handling such disputes.

4.2 This chapter examines the leading cases in detail, drawing out key themes, analysing judicial reasoning, and illustrating the constraints under which courts operate. It also considers unreported but widely discussed county court decisions, the way these cases reflect broader legal principles, and the extent to which case law sheds light on the future direction of reform.

4.3 Before analysing individual authorities, it is important to understand why so few judgments exist. First, pet disputes are often emotionally intense but financially low-value. Courts therefore encourage settlement, viewing contested hearings as disproportionate in the context of judicial resources. In many financial remedy hearings, a pet dispute may arise only briefly on the margins of broader issues and may be resolved through last-minute negotiation or pragmatic compromise.

4.4 Second, the legal principles are straightforward, even if emotionally unsatisfactory. Because pets are classified as personal property, disputes turn on conventional ownership analysis. Judges seldom consider such cases to raise novel points of law warranting publication.

4.5 Third, judges are wary of creating precedent that could encourage litigation. Published judgments can signal to the public that certain arguments are viable, unintentionally inviting more disputes to enter the court system. Given the pressures on family courts, most judges prefer to resolve pet issues quietly, proportionately, and without reported authority.

4.6 Nevertheless, several decisions stand out as touchstones in this area. They highlight how judges apply property law to living beings and provide a framework for practitioners advising clients.

Glaister-Carlisle v Glaister-Carlisle[1]

4.7 One of the most frequently cited cases in the context of pets on divorce is *Glaister-Carlisle v Glaister-Carlisle* (1968). Although not strictly a divorce case, it is foundational in determining how courts analyse disputes over the ownership of animals.

4.8 In *Glaister-Carlisle*, the dispute centred on whether a dog had been gifted by the husband to the wife. The Court of Appeal reaffirmed classical principles governing gifts of personal property: intention, delivery, and acceptance. A valid gift requires that:

1. the donor intends to give the item away permanently;

---

1 [1968] 112 SJ 215

2. the item is delivered to the donee; and
3. the donee accepts the gift.

4.9 The wife in this case argued that the dog had been given to her during the marriage. The husband disputed this, asserting that he had merely allowed her to care for it. The Court of Appeal found that ambiguous statements, affectionate references, or conduct consistent with shared enjoyment were insufficient to establish a clear intention to transfer ownership.

4.10 This judgment has had a lasting influence. It demonstrates that courts require clarity and objective evidence when determining whether ownership was transferred. A passing remark such as "the dog is really yours" is unlikely to suffice unless supported by delivery of the animal and a demonstrable intention to relinquish control.

4.11 For practitioners, the case underscores the difficulty of arguing that a pet was gifted absent explicit evidence. Clients often believe that emotional or relational context birthdays, anniversaries, meaningful life events should influence the analysis. While relevant, these factors are rarely decisive in court.

4.12 The case also demonstrates the judiciary's reluctance to infer a transfer of ownership from domestic behaviour. This is an important point: cohabiting couples routinely share responsibilities for pets without articulating ownership. *Glaister-Carlisle* warns that courts will not readily impose a legal meaning onto emotional or relational actions.

S v S[2]

4.13 This case concerns the appeal of the Respondent, husband, against an Order which was made by District Judge Segal on 3 May 2007.

4.14 The husband advanced a position within the proceedings that he was intending to leave his city job in the next one to five years and that he wished to live in the country and retrain for a new job, possibly working with animals.

4.15 The wife's position was that she had already given the best years of her career to her eleven-year marriage and that she could not significantly increase her earning capacity. Her horses were a key factor in her position regarding the standard of living she enjoyed during the marriage she sought a property in Gloucestershire with enough land to house her and her two horses.

4.16 Paragraph 12 of the original judgment was highlighted on appeal, as follows:

> *"In any event, the wife does not want a 9-5 job, because this would not give her enough time with her horses. I am not qualified to say whether or not it is because she has no children that she is so devoted to her horses, but it is clear that she is devoted to them. She said: "Horses are my family. I see them every day. When the older ones see me they whinny at me. You form a very close bond with horses". The husband very fairly said: "I agree that her major activity outside work is her horses".*
>
> *"During the marriage, the horses plainly played a major part in the wife's life with the consent and encouragement of the husband. All the more so, after she lost a baby in 2001 and the husband gave her a third horse (a foal), to celebrate their*

2 [2008] EWHC 519 (Fam)

10th Wedding Anniversary in 2004, to add to her own two horses, which she had bought herself for £20,000 out of a personal inheritance in order to develop her eventing. It was the husband's case that, on break up of the marriage, the horses were an unjustified extravagance and that the wife's housing needs could be properly satisfied by purchase of a house which had no facilities to keep horses for about £600,000, and that she should keep one horse only which could be put out to livery while she worked a full time week. The wife, on the other hand, (who did not accept that £600,000 was enough in any event and whose rejection of the examples of houses produced by the husband in that price bracket the judge appears to have accepted) wished to keep her three horses. The husband conceded that, whether the wife had two or three horses, it was cheaper to keep them at home with a full time groom than to put them out to livery. The wife did not in fact claim for the cost of a full time groom. On the basis that she only worked part time, her claim in respect of the cost of her three horses only included a part time helper. There were thus two competing "packages" of proposals. The wife's case was that she should be permitted to keep up her life style with horses so long as the husband's means permitted, and the husband's case was that there should be an immediate change to a long term pattern, whereby the wife's previously consuming interest and activity in eventing should be abandoned in favour of a requirement to take a full time job, maintaining a single horse simply for the purpose of weekend recreation and exercise. The District Judge accepted the package put forward by the wife as constituting the fair solution, so long as the husband's income level was maintained".

RK v RK[3]

4.17 This case provides one of the most detailed modern discussions of pet ownership within financial remedy proceedings. The case involved two dogs whose ownership was disputed following the breakdown of the marriage. The wife argued that she was the primary caregiver and that the dogs should remain with her. The husband asserted ownership based on purchase and documentation.

4.18 The High Court found for the husband, relying primarily on evidence of legal ownership and financial responsibility. The judgment is frequently cited for its clear articulation of the principle that emotional attachment and care do not equate to legal ownership. In the judgment no information in respect of the dog is provided, save for the following sentence at paragraph 85:

> *'On the latter issue, I do not consider it appropriate to make any order in respect of one of the dogs because, on the evidence I have heard, they would seem to have been looked after principally by the husband.'*

Conversely, there are four paragraphs dealing with the paintings.

4.19 Despite acknowledging the wife's strong emotional bond with the dogs and her role in their daily care, the court concluded that the legal evidence of ownership was overwhelming.

4.20 The judgment also rejected the idea of shared care. The wife proposed an arrangement whereby the dogs would spend alternating weeks with each party. The court declined to make such an order, emphasising concerns about enforceability and the desire for finality. The judge noted that shared-care orders for pets were inappropriate in the

---

[3] [2011] EWHC 3910 (Fam)

absence of a statutory welfare framework and risked generating ongoing conflict.

4.21 Several themes emerge from *RK v RK*:

- Judges often express sympathy for the emotional significance of pets but cannot treat emotional attachment as a legal basis for ownership.

- Insurance records, adoption documents, microchip information, and veterinary registrations carried significant weight. Even if such documents reflected administrative roles rather than caregiving, they formed the backbone of the court's reasoning.

- The judgment reflects the judiciary's consistent unwillingness to create arrangements requiring continued cooperation between separated parties.

IX v IY[4]

4.22 In *this case*, the court faced a situation involving two dogs. Ownership of both dogs was unclear. The court ultimately awarded one dog to each party, emphasising pragmatic considerations and the need to reach a swift, final resolution.

Although emotionally unsatisfactory, the decision reflects judicial priorities:

- avoid ongoing disputes,

---

4 (Financial Remedies: Unmatched Contributions) [2018] EWHC 3053 (Fam)

- reduce opportunities for post-order conflict,
- achieve finality in proceedings,
- resolve low-value issues proportionately.

4.23 The judgment is notable for acknowledging the emotional impact of separating bonded animals while nevertheless concluding that the court's task is not to apply a welfare test. The judge made clear that the court cannot apply a "best interests of the animal" analysis, even if such a test would produce a more humane outcome.

In resolution of this dispute, Moylan LJ said:

> *"I have heard almost nothing on this issue although I believe that one dog is currently in France and one dog is in England. That seems to me to be fair. If the parties wish to argue over their access to the other dog I would suggest that they place the dispute before a mediator or arbitrator; perhaps one with experience of dogs."*

KV v KV[5]

4.24 This case concerns the wife's application for maintenance pending suit (under section 22 of the Matrimonial Causes Act 1973) and a Legal Services Payments Order (under section 22ZA of the same Act). The parties began cohabiting in 2004, married in 2009 and they separated in 2021. There was a dispute about jurisdiction and whilst the wife's financial remedy application could not be pursued until this was resolved, the court dealt with the interim financial issued, pending the hearing to resolve the jurisdiction/forum dispute. One of the relevant applications was the interim application issued on 14 May 2024 seeking:

---

5 [2024] EWFC 165

1) the return of the child following a holiday in the Caribbean to England and 2) for the delivery up of several horses who had been diverted on the way home from a competition.

4.25 The application in respect of the horses was adjourned to a further hearing. The costs of litigating on the dispute arising from the horses, was not factored into the wife's LSPO application. The wife's total claimed costs, including VAT and disbursements, and not including the costs to litigate regarding the horses stood at £1,068,109.

4.26 For the MPS application, the wife's budget was £4,579,290 for herself and £515,070 for the children. The husband was ordered to pay all of the costs relating to the horses. This was a total of £1,145,200pa, which included £85,000pa for staff.

FI v DO[6]

4.27 This is a first instance decision by District Judge Crisp, sitting in Manchester, who was dealing with the financial claims arising from a 12 year marriage. There were two children, who at the time of the hearing were living with their mother. They were having no contact with their father. There was a family dog, whom the husband had made an application seeking a shared care arrangement and declaration of ownership.

4.28 The wife initially sought for the family dog to be in her care but for the dog to travel with the children to the husband's home and for him to have contact, if the court allowed it. The wife's position changed, following an incident on 12 December 2022 and did not think it was in the dog's best interests to spend time with the husband.

6 [2024] EWFC 384 (B) (20 December 2024)

4.29 The husband advanced an argument that he suffered from anxiety and depression which impacts his day-to-day activities and that this is a long-term condition which qualifies as a disability under the Equality Act. The husband's position was that he purchased the family dog for £1,200 cash and that the wife did not make any financial contribution. He stated that he trained the dog and registered her with as a Disability Support dog to assist him with his anxiety and depression. He said after their separation, the wife did not walk or feed the dog and he became her sole carer.

4.30 The husband's position regarding the incident on 12 December 2022 was that he was visiting his previous dog's grave and saw a dog running freely in the area. He took the dog and she was happy to go with him. He was then arrested by the police later on, who removed the dog and returned her to the wife.

4.31 During cross examination, the husband said he was exercising his legal rights, as he had more rights than the grandmother who was walking the dog at the time. This is why he took her. He accepted the dog ran off back to the family home but denies dragging her. He was very firm that it was his dog as he paid for it.

4.32 The wife's position was that the family dog was purchased jointly. She contributed £280, her daughter used £320 of her birthday money, and the husband paid the balance of £600. The reason for the purchase of the dog was that the children were distraught from the loss of their previous dog. The wife was her registered keeper; she was registered at the Kennel Club and the wife paid for all of her veterinary bills and insurance etc.

4.33 The wife did not accept that the family dog was registered as a Disability Support dog for the husband. In respect of the incident on 12 December 2022, the wife received a distressed call from her 72 year old mother, who was out walking the dog, to say that the dog has run off as the father was chasing her and she recorded the husband dragging the dog into his car from the family home, where the dog had run back to.

The husband was arrested and reported to the RSPCA and the dog was returned to the wife, with damaged paws due to being dragged away by the husband.

4.34 It had been 18 months since the family dog had seen the husband and the wife's position was that she did not recognise him due to the significant passing of time.

4.35 District Judge Crisp referred to the case of *RK v RK*[7] *[2011] EWHC 3907 (Fam) Moylan J*, in relation to the dog:

> *"I do not consider it appropriate to make any order in respect of one of the dogs, because on the evidence I have heard, they would seem to have been principally looked after by the husband".*

Regarding her findings of fact, District Judge Crisp stated:

> *"Both parties gave evidence which veered off the point at times albeit I accept that both are upset, and the husband does have a mental health disability. It has not helped this case that such a level of information was put before the court about who paid for the dog and who owned the dog. As I said during their evidence it matters not who paid for the dog. The dog is a chattel. At times it seemed to me that I was in the realms of a Children Act application which featured the dog when the wife was cross examined about the dog's welfare and shared care arrangements. I set this out because I have no doubt that if this feature could have been agreed other matters may have been able to be agreed."*

4.36 District Judge Crisp found that the first registration of the dog as a disability dog was in February 2024. Further, in respect of the civil application that the husband had made regarding the dog, the letter

---

7 [2011] EWHC 3907 (Fam) / RK (n 3)

before action written in January 2024 did not ask for the return of the dog on the basis that she was a support dog. It stated that he wishes for her to be delivered up or a shared care arrangement to be in place, and he made a civil claim in respect of for £39,600 for the loss of litters during her lifetime. The Judge found that the facts did not support the husband's position that the family dog was purchased as a disability dog, rather that the husband simply viewed her as an income stream.

4.37 In respect of who purchased the dog, the Judge accepted the wife's evidence that both the wife and their child contributed towards the joint purchase of the family dog. The letter before action written by the husband also stated, "*On the 30th of May 2022.....jointly purchased a female Golden Retriever*" and he also demanded the parties jointly contributed towards matrimonial outgoings, which fits with this position.

4.38 In her judgment, District Judge Crisp stated that the issue of the family dog was a '*thorny*' one. She found the wife's evidence compelling and did not accept that the husband did not take the dog forcibly, as he suggested. She further stated that the father failed to see the implications of his actions which impacted the family (in particular the grandmother and children) and:

> *"I also do not accept his evidence that the wife did not care for the dog after they separated, her evidence was far more in tune with someone who has the welfare of the dog at heart."*

4.39 District Judge Crisp referred again to the case of RK v RK in that this legal authority provides assistance in who principally looked after the dog. It did not deal with who purchased the dog. She states "*that fact in my view is not as important as who the dog sees as her carer. This is not who had previously looked after the dog, but who does now.*" She accepted that the wife cared for the dog 18 months since separation, that the dog considered the family home as a safe place to live which is why she ran back there after the husband tried to take her. The Judge found the wife compelling regarding her understanding of dogs, that she was compassionate and would put the dog's interests first. Ultimately it was ordered that the "dog's home is with the wife, and she should stay there".

4.40 Beyond the reported cases, numerous unreported decisions shape practitioners' understanding of how courts approach these disputes. Although such decisions lack formal precedential value, the consistency of their reasoning reinforces the principles already discussed.

Across the country, district judges have:

- declined to order shared care for pets;
- awarded ownership based on documentation even where caregiving rested predominantly with the other party;
- separated multiple pets to avoid joint ownership;
- encouraged parties to resolve disputes through mediation;
- emphasised that the court cannot adjudicate on welfare or emotional factors.

4.41 These practical realities are critical for practitioners. They clarify what arguments will and will not gain traction and highlight the importance of gathering strong ownership evidence early in proceedings.

4.42 Although sparse, the available case law reveals several recurring themes:

- Every judgment begins and ends with the question of legal ownership. Emotional factors may be referenced sympathetically but are not determinative.
- Courts rely heavily on paperwork. This creates both opportunities and challenges for clients. The party with stronger

documentary evidence often prevails, even if caregiving responsibilities suggest a different outcome.

- Unlike children, pets do not benefit from a statutory welfare test. Courts cannot consider what outcome would be "best" for the animal.

- Judges consistently emphasise enforcement difficulties and the need for finality.

- Decisions sometimes reflect practical considerations rather than strictly doctrinal ones, particularly in cases involving multiple pets.

- While judges apply the law as written, several judgments hint at discomfort, noting the gap between social expectations and legal classification.

4.43 The reported and unreported cases collectively reveal a legal framework that is increasingly out of step with modern family life. Clients expect disputes involving beloved pets to be handled with sensitivity to welfare, emotional attachment and practical realities. Judges, constrained by statute and doctrine, can offer none of these.

The cases highlight:

- the limitations of property law when applied to sentient beings;

- the potential injustice of decisions based solely on ownership;

- the inadequacy of current remedies for parties seeking shared arrangements;

- the emotional harm caused by rigid legal structures;

- the urgent need for coherent statutory guidance.

4.44 These themes provide the foundation for emerging reform proposals and for the work of the Working Group on Pets on Divorce & Separation, discussed later in Chapter 10.

CHAPTER FIVE

PROPERTY ADJUSTMENT ORDERS

5.1 Under section 24 of the Matrimonial Causes Act 1973, a court may make orders transferring property between spouses. These powers apply to all forms of property, including pets, which are therefore treated as chattels capable of being transferred by judicial order.

5.2 Although clients often expect the court to make detailed orders about "custody" or "care" of a pet, such orders fall outside the statutory framework. A property adjustment order can:

- transfer legal and beneficial ownership of a pet from one spouse to another;
- resolve disputes over title;
- ensure clarity around responsibility for the animal post-separation.

5.3 However, the order cannot, as a matter of principle:

- impose ongoing shared-care arrangements,
- create contact schedules,
- require cooperation between the parties,
- incorporate welfare considerations akin to child arrangements,
- mandate future decision-making protocols about the pet.

5.4 The distinction is crucial. The court's powers extend only to the allocation of the pet as property. Everything else must be achieved through private agreement or non-court dispute resolution.

Timing

5.5 One of the biggest obstacles in pet disputes is delay. Practitioners often focus initially on larger issues such as housing needs, pensions, income, maintenance, and address pet matters later. This can create several problems:

5.6 Clients may become entrenched if uncertainty persists, particularly where a pet resides temporarily with one party. If a pet remains with one person during separation, it may be harder to argue for transfer later, especially if the other party appears disengaged.

5.7 Agreements that might have been possible at an early stage may become unworkable once trust erodes.

Practitioners should therefore identify pet-related issues at the outset, gathering evidence early and tackling pet disputes alongside financial negotiations.

Drafting Consent Orders

5.8 Consent orders involving pets must be unambiguous. Vague or incomplete drafting can lead to misunderstandings, enforcement problems, or even post-order litigation. When drafting, practitioners should consider incorporating the following elements:

Identification of the Pet

5.9 A consent order should begin by clearly identifying the pet, including:

- name,
- species,
- breed,
- date of birth or approximate age,
- microchip number (for clarity, even though not determinative of ownership),
- any distinguishing characteristics.

Precise identification helps avoid disputes, particularly if multiple pets are involved.

Transfer of legal and beneficial ownership

5.6 The language must expressly transfer both legal and beneficial ownership:

> "*The [dog/cat], 'X', shall be transferred to the [husband/wife], who shall thereafter hold sole legal and beneficial ownership of X.*"

This avoids ambiguity about whether the arrangement is temporary or whether any residual rights remain with the other party.

Responsibility for microchip, insurance and veterinary records

5.7 Although microchip registration does not determine ownership, courts and practitioners recognise its practical importance. Orders should specify:

- who must update the microchip database;
- who will be listed as owner on veterinary records;
- responsibility for insurance premiums;
- responsibility for ongoing medical decision-making.

Transitional arrangements

5.8 Transitional arrangements should not be placed in the operative part of the order, as they are unenforceable and may create ongoing obligations. Instead, they should be documented in:

- a recital,
- or a side letter between solicitors,
- or a mediation/arbitration agreement.

Transitional provisions might include:

- time for the non-owner to say goodbye to the pet;
- a phased introduction of the pet to new surroundings;
- agreement to share veterinary information during the transition.

Financial considerations

5.9 If the pet has significant monetary value, such as a pedigree show dog, breeding animal, or trained assistance animal, the order may need to address:

- valuation,
- financial adjustment or compensation,
- division of income from breeding (rare but not unheard of),
- arrangements for future costs related to specialist care.

Costs of transfer

5.10 Parties should clarify who bears the costs of transfer, including transport, veterinary checks, or equipment.

Dealing with multiple pets

5.11 Disputes involving multiple pets introduce additional complexity, particularly where animals are bonded or where ownership is unclear.

While courts sometimes divide pets between parties, this may cause emotional distress. Private agreements are more flexible and can prioritise welfare.

In some relationships, each partner may have stronger ties to particular animals. Identifying these distinctions can assist negotiation. For example, an elderly dog may require a quieter home, while a younger dog may need more exercise.

Clear drafting is essential where multiple pets are assigned to different parties to avoid confusion.

Drafting side letters and informal agreements

5.12 Although unenforceable, side letters can be invaluable, reflecting a level of goodwill that may help the parties function more cooperatively post-separation. Common elements of side letters include:

- agreed visiting arrangements,
- shared walking schedules,
- agreements about holidays,
- commitments to consult on major medical decisions,
- flexible arrangements during illness or emergencies.

Practitioners should, however, clearly explain to clients that these arrangements cannot be enforced by the court. Their value lies in the goodwill between parties and the desire to preserve stability for the pet, not in legal enforceability.

Side letters can also defuse tension: agreeing a compassionate transition often allows the legally "losing" party to feel heard and respected, reducing the emotional sting of the formal order.

Drafting in cases of high conflict

5.13 Some pet disputes arise in high-conflict separations where cooperation is unlikely. In such cases, drafting must be especially clear and cautious. Practitioners should:

- Avoid shared care language. Shared arrangements invite dispute. If a party insists on such arrangements, practitioners should stress the risks and direct them to alternatives such as mediation or arbitration.

- Consider protective measures. Where one party has exhibited controlling behaviour, harming or threatening to remove the pet may form part of a coercive pattern. Practitioners should consider whether a non-molestation order or safeguarding referrals are appropriate.

- Address the risk of removal. Orders may include a recital that neither party shall remove the pet from a specified address prior to transfer, though enforcement challenges remain.

- Document instances of abuse or neglect. While welfare is not a legal test, evidential concerns about neglect or aggression may influence pragmatic judicial decisions where ownership is unclear.

Drafting in mediation and arbitration

5.14 Non-court dispute resolution is particularly suited to pet disputes because mediators and arbitrators are not constrained by the property classification. They can craft bespoke arrangements including shared care or welfare-based provisions.

Mediation

5.15 Mediation encourages open discussion and offers space for parties to articulate emotional concerns. Mediated agreements can:

- preserve the pet's routine;

- allow the non-owner to maintain contact;

- include welfare-focused provisions;

- adapt over time.

Practitioners should prepare clients by helping them identify their underlying needs, often emotional rather than ownership-based, before entering mediation.

Arbitration

5.16 Arbitration is a powerful option because:

- the arbitrator can consider welfare and emotional factors;
- outcomes are binding;
- the process is private and faster than court;
- arrangements can be bespoke and detailed.

Many clients prefer arbitration because their animals' welfare can be discussed openly without legal constraints.

The Importance of clear communication with clients

5.17 Drafting cannot occur effectively without careful communication. Clients experiencing the emotional turmoil of separation may struggle to process the legal distinction between ownership and welfare. Practitioners play a crucial role in managing expectations, which helps avoid protracted disputes.

Key points to explain include:

- pets are legally property;
- courts cannot make shared-care orders;

- ownership evidence is crucial;
- informal agreements may be possible even if the court cannot impose them;
- early negotiation is preferable to litigation;
- arbitration and mediation offer greater flexibility.

Clear, sensitive communication prevents misunderstandings and builds trust at a time when clients may feel vulnerable and overwhelmed.

5.18 Despite skilful drafting, some disputes cannot be resolved because parties fundamentally disagree on ownership or emotional entitlement. In such cases, litigation may be unavoidable. Practitioners should then:

- assemble comprehensive ownership evidence;
- consider whether interim arrangements are needed;
- guide clients through likely outcomes;
- prepare for the possibility that the court may allocate the pet based on documentation alone.

Understanding the limits of drafting is vital: drafting is a tool, not a remedy for the emotional complexities underlying pet disputes.

5.20 Property adjustment orders offer a narrow but essential mechanism for resolving pet disputes on divorce. Although the statutory framework is limited, effective drafting, supported by clear communication, early identification of issues, and strategic use of non-court processes, can mitigate many of the challenges inherent in these cases. Practitioners who understand the constraints, anticipate emotional flashpoints, and draft with clarity can help clients achieve more humane, stable and durable outcomes.

This foundation sets the stage for an in-depth consideration of non-court dispute resolution, explored in Chapter 7.

CHAPTER SIX

MANAGING CLIENT EXPECTATIONS

6.1 Disputes about pets on divorce often present a unique challenge for family lawyers. While legally modest, they are frequently among the most emotionally charged issues in a case. Clients may be pragmatic and realistic about finances yet become deeply entrenched when it comes to a dog, cat or other companion animal. The combination of intense emotional attachment and a restrictive legal framework requires careful strategy, rigorous evidence management, and clear client communication.

6.2 This chapter examines how practitioners can approach pet disputes strategically, how to identify and deploy relevant evidence effectively, and how to manage client expectations in a way that reduces conflict and promotes resolution.

Understanding the emotional landscape

6.3 Before strategy or evidence can be addressed, it is essential to recognise the emotional context in which pet disputes arise. For many clients, a pet represents continuity, comfort and identity at a time of profound upheaval. Losing a pet may feel like losing the last stable element of family life. This explains why pet disputes can provoke responses that appear disproportionate to their financial value.

For practitioners, acknowledging this emotional reality is not a concession of legal ground. On the contrary, it is often a prerequisite to dispensing effective advice. Clients who feel dismissed or misunderstood are more likely to litigate irrationally. A client who feels heard is more likely to accept legal limitations and engage constructively in proceedings.

Identifying the real issue

6.4 A key strategic step is identifying what the client actually wants. While clients may frame their position in terms of ownership or "custody", their underlying concern may be different. Common underlying drivers include:

- fear of losing daily companionship;
- concern about the pet's welfare in the other party's care;
- a sense of injustice or lack of recognition for caregiving;
- anxiety about further loss following separation;
- desire for leverage in wider negotiations.

Understanding these motivations allows the practitioner to tailor advice and strategy. For example, a client whose primary concern is reassurance about welfare may be more open to mediated arrangements or informal agreements than to contested litigation over ownership.

Evidence

6.5 Because pets are treated as chattels, evidence relating to ownership is paramount. One of the practitioner's most important tasks is to help clients understand the difference between emotionally compelling evidence and legally relevant evidence.

Core ownership evidence

6.6 The following categories of evidence are routinely compelling:

- Purchase or adoption documentation: breeder contracts, adoption agreements or receipts often carry significant weight, particularly where only one party is named.
- Microchip registration: while not determinative of ownership, microchip records form part of the evidential picture and are often relied upon by courts.
- Veterinary and insurance records: these documents may indicate responsibility and involvement, though they often reflect administrative convenience rather than ownership.
- Financial evidence: payment for purchase, insurance, food, veterinary care or training can support an ownership claim, especially where consistent over time.
- Evidence of intention: correspondence or contemporaneous documents showing how the parties understood ownership at the time of acquisition.

Practitioners should gather this evidence early. Delay can lead to lost documents, fading recollections and increased entrenchment.

Evidence with limited legal value

6.7 By contrast, clients often place weight on evidence that is legally weak or irrelevant, such as:

- the strength of emotional attachment;
- the pet's apparent preference;

- the amount of time spent caregiving;
- statements from friends or family about the client's bond with the pet.

While such evidence may be relevant in mediation or arbitration, it is unlikely to determine the outcome in court. Practitioners must explain this distinction clearly, while remaining sensitive to the client's feelings.

Timing and interim arrangements

6.8 Timing is often decisive in pet disputes. Where a pet remains living with one party post-separation, that arrangement can become entrenched, particularly if proceedings are delayed. Courts may be reluctant to disrupt an established status quo, even where ownership evidence is contested.

Practitioners should therefore consider pet arrangements at the earliest possible stage, ideally alongside initial financial discussions. Interim agreements, even if informal, can prevent unilateral action and reduce the risk of escalation.

Managing expectations

6.9 Managing client expectations is arguably the most challenging aspect of pet disputes. Many clients approach these cases with assumptions that do not align with the law, including beliefs that:

- the court will prioritise the pet's welfare;
- caregiving will outweigh ownership;
- shared-care arrangements are likely;

- the court can impose contact arrangements.

None of these assumptions reflect current legal reality. Practitioners must explain from the outset that the court's powers are limited and that litigation may not deliver the outcome the client hopes for.

The manner in which this advice is delivered matters. A blunt recitation of legal principles can feel dismissive. A more effective approach is to acknowledge the client's emotional position, explain the legal framework clearly, and then refocus the discussion on achievable outcomes.

Use of non-court dispute resolution

6.10 Given the limitations of litigation, strategy in pet disputes should almost always involve consideration of non-court dispute resolution. Mediation and arbitration offer flexibility that the court lacks, allowing welfare, routine and emotional attachment to be explored openly.

6.11 Practitioners should present NCDR not as a compromise or second-best option, but as the forum most likely to produce an agreed and workable outcome. This is particularly important where the client's goals include shared care, ongoing contact or welfare-based arrangements that the court cannot order.

Pets are sometimes used, consciously or unconsciously, as leverage in wider financial negotiations. While this may be tactically tempting, it carries significant risks. Escalating a pet dispute can harden positions, prolong proceedings and damage prospects for settlement on more substantial issues.

Practitioners should be alert to situations where a pet is being used as a proxy for unresolved emotional conflict or as a bargaining chip. Clear advice about proportionality, costs and likely outcomes is essential to prevent such disputes from spiralling.

High-conflict and safeguarding cases

6.12 In cases involving high conflict, coercive control or allegations of abuse, pet disputes require particular care. Pets may be used as a means of control or intimidation, and threats to remove or harm an animal can form part of a wider pattern of behaviour.

In such cases, practitioners should prioritise safety, consider whether protective orders are appropriate, and be cautious about promoting shared arrangements or NCDR processes that may expose the client or the pet to risk.

Clarity is key

6.13 Ultimately, effective strategy in pet disputes rests on clarity: clarity about the law, about evidence, and about what outcomes are realistically achievable. By combining rigorous evidence analysis with sensitive expectation management, practitioners can reduce conflict, protect their clients' interests, and guide families towards outcomes that, while not perfect, are stable and humane.

Pets may be treated as property in law, but disputes about them are rarely just about ownership. The family lawyer's task is to navigate that tension with professionalism, judgment and care.

CHAPTER SEVEN

NON-COURT DISPUTE RESOLUTION

7.1 Non-court dispute resolution (NCDR) plays an increasingly central role in family justice, and pet disputes are one of the clearest examples of why the system is shifting away from litigation. Because the courts are constrained by the treatment of pets as chattels, and because judicial remedies are limited, blunt, and often emotionally unsatisfying, NCDR offers a space where parties can explore solutions that courts simply cannot entertain.

7.2 This chapter provides a detailed examination of mediation, arbitration, collaborative law, and solicitor-led negotiation in the context of pet disputes, alongside practical advice for preparing clients, structuring agreements, and managing risk. It also examines recent changes to the Family Procedure Rules (FPR) and the policy context in which NCDR is encouraged, even expected, by judges.

7.3 As mentioned above, pre-emptive legal steps can help to prevent distress and costs of dealing with any pet related issues. Incorporating a clause in a Pet-Nup to prioritise NCDR can also encourage the parties to resolve any future disputes outside of the process, focusing on their pets' best interests.

7.4 Under the Family Procedure Rules (FPR) (3.3(1A)), introduced in April 2024, parties to proceedings are required to set out their views on using NCDR as a means of resolution. The form FM5 is to be filed and exchanged at least seven days before the first appointment. Failure to engage in NCDR, can significantly impact costs, under FPR 28.3(6) and 28.3(7), if the courts deem it appropriate for the parties to engage in NCDR.

7.5 The rules have been amended to consider non-attendance at a Mediation Information and Assessment Meeting (MIAM) or lack of lack of participation in NCDR as conduct, impacting costs.

7.6 Early discussions between the parties, can assist with the parties having open conversations about any disputes in respect of custody of a pet, in the hope to avoid last minute, highly emotional disputes. If matters are still unable to be resolved, then mediation and arbitration are viable options, as these will emphasise the welfare of the pet, over legal ownership disputes.

7.7 Arbitration can provide a bespoke approach to resolving disputes in respect of pets. Under the Arbitration Rules of the Family Law Arbitration Scheme (ARB1FS), parties can set out the specifics of their disputes, which they need assistance with. An experienced arbitrator who specifically deals with pets can be engaged and agreeing to arbitrate, means that costs can be awarded against a person who unreasonably refuses to engage in the process. This would amount to litigation conduct, under FPR 28.3(7). This would prove to be extremely useful, in cases where a person has failed to arbitrate, following an agreement to do so, within the drafting of the Pet-Nup.

7.8 Pet disputes present a unique combination of factors that make litigation not only unsuitable but often counterproductive:

The law provides limited remedies

7.9 The court's powers are confined to determining ownership. It cannot:

- impose shared-care arrangements;
- create detailed routines or schedules;
- consider the pet's welfare;

- make ongoing supervisory orders.

NCDR, by contrast, is unconstrained. Mediators and arbitrators can consider welfare, emotional attachment, routine, behavioural patterns, and the needs of the animal.

Emotional intensity is high

7.10 Clients may express more anguish over losing a pet than over financial issues. Litigation tends to harden positions; NCDR allows acknowledgement, empathy and creative problem-solving.

Parties often want ongoing flexibility

7.11 Even where ownership is transferred, parties may wish to maintain limited contact or receive updates. Courts cannot accommodate these wishes; NCDR can.

Costs of litigation are disproportionate

7.12 A contested dispute over a dog or cat can easily exceed the animal's monetary value. NCDR is quicker, cheaper and more humane. Judges regularly indicate that pet disputes should be resolved privately unless absolutely unavoidable.

Mediation

7.13 Mediation is often the most constructive forum for resolving pet disputes. Unlike litigation, mediation allows parties to articulate emotional needs, explore welfare-focused outcomes, and design a plan that balances attachment, routine, and stability.

How mediation works in pet disputes

7.14 A trained mediator—often with family law or therapeutic expertise—facilitates discussion. Mediation sessions allow parties to:

- express their emotional connection to the pet;
- discuss the animal's routine and needs;
- identify what each person fears losing;
- explore different care or ownership options;
- consider the long-term implications of different arrangements.

Because mediation is future-focused, parties are encouraged to look beyond the legal rigidity of ownership and consider what outcomes feel humane, stable and respectful.

Mediation allows for a range of solutions unavailable in court, such as:

- Shared-care arrangements (e.g., alternate weekends, split holidays);
- Flexible time-limited contact (e.g., final farewell visits or occasional walks);
- Joint decision-making for major medical issues;
- Behavioural support plans;
- Financial sharing (insurance, food, training);
- Routine-preservation plans (minimising disruption for the animal).

Many separating couples find that once they have space to articulate their needs, a compromise becomes possible, often one that reflects the animal's welfare.

Benefits of mediation

- Less adversarial;
- Cheaper than litigation;
- Faster;
- More emotionally supportive;
- Retains party autonomy;
- Allows solutions that align with the animal's welfare.

Limitations

- Not legally binding unless converted into a formal agreement;
- Requires a baseline level of goodwill;
- May not be suitable in high-conflict or coercive-control cases.

Nevertheless, mediation remains the single most effective forum for addressing pet disputes in the majority of cases.

Arbitration

7.15 Arbitration has become increasingly popular in family law, and its benefits are especially pronounced in pet disputes. Unlike mediators, arbitrators can impose binding decisions, yet they enjoy flexibility that judges in statutory courts cannot.

Arbitrators can:

- consider the welfare of the animal;
- examine emotional factors;
- make bespoke arrangements;
- tailor outcomes to reflect bonding, routine and behavioural needs;
- structure shared-care agreements, if appropriate;
- create gradual transition periods;
- make decisions more quickly than courts.

Crucially, arbitration decisions are binding. Parties therefore gain both flexibility and certainty.

Types of arrangements an arbitrator can make

Examples include:

- awarding ownership but providing for a time-limited transition period;
- requiring the owner to give the other party regular updates;

- setting out agreed behavioural training steps;
- designing a structured shared-care regime;
- agreeing financial contributions for pet-related expenses.

Although not enforceable in the same manner as contact arrangements for children, arbitration agreements are binding.

Choosing the right arbitrator

Practitioners should consider:

- arbitrators with experience in welfare, animal behaviour or complex emotional disputes;
- arbitrators trained through the Institute of Family Law Arbitrators (IFLA);
- arbitrators respected for balanced, sensitive decision-making.

Advantages over court

- Privacy
- Speed
- Flexibility
- Ability to adopt welfare-based reasoning
- Reduced conflict
- Greater creativity

For many families, arbitration achieves outcomes that feel fairer, kinder and more reflective of the animal's needs.

Collaborative law

7.16 Collaborative law is another effective NCDR method. In a collaborative process, both parties and their solicitors commit to resolving matters without litigation. Meetings involve open discussion, shared information and problem-solving.

Collaborative practitioners can:

- bring in animal behaviourists;
- consult veterinary experts;
- explore emotional impact through therapeutic tools;
- craft nuanced care arrangements;
- manage communication breakdowns.

This interdisciplinary method can be particularly helpful when both parties feel strongly attached to the pet and wish to minimise conflict.

Advantages

- Supportive, structured environment;
- Multidisciplinary input;
- Tailored solutions;
- Long-term focus;

- Reduced hostility.

Limitations

- Not suitable where trust has broken down completely;
- Can be expensive in complex cases;
- Requires commitment from both solicitors.

Solicitor-led negotiation

7.17 Most pet disputes resolve through solicitor-to-solicitor negotiation. This may involve:

- correspondence;
- without-prejudice proposals;
- round-table meetings;
- hybrid mediation;
- early neutral evaluation.

Practitioners should:

- gather ownership evidence early;
- identify what outcome their client truly seeks;
- explore emotional motivations;
- understand the other party's drivers;

- propose creative solutions even where the law cannot impose them.

Managing client expectations

Solicitors must explain early:

- the difference between legal ownership and caregiving;
- the impossibility of court-ordered shared care;
- the risks of litigation;
- the benefits of mediated or negotiated compromise.

Clients often cling to the hope that the court will recognise their emotional bond with the pet. Sensitive but clear explanation prevents later disappointment.

The Impact of the Family Procedure Rules (FPR)

7.18 Recent amendments to the Family Procedure Rules reinforce the expectation that parties engage with NCDR before turning to litigation.

MIAM requirements

7.19 Parties must usually attend a Mediation Information and Assessment Meeting unless exempt. Although many clients initially resist mediation, MIAMs provide an opportunity to explore whether pet issues could be resolved in a more humane forum.

Court scrutiny of NCDR engagement

7.20 Judges increasingly ask:

- "Why has mediation not been attempted?"
- "Have parties considered arbitration?"
- "Why was negotiation insufficient?"

A refusal to engage in NCDR can lead to adverse cost consequences. Judges generally take the view that pet disputes should be resolved through negotiation or NCDR wherever possible.

Preparing clients for NCDR

7.21 To be effective, practitioners must prepare clients carefully.

Clients may fear losing:

- companionship,
- routine,
- a sense of purpose,
- a "family member",
- continuity for children.

Understanding these drivers helps shape negotiation.

Clients often assume they have stronger "rights" because they were the primary caregiver. Practitioners must explain that caregiving does not automatically create legal ownership.

Encourage clients to consider:

- the pet's routine,
- the risk of ongoing conflict,
- the feasibility of shared arrangements,
- the value of certainty

A client who understands mediation, arbitration and collaborative law is more likely to choose a constructive path.

Drafting NCDR Agreements

7.22 Agreements should be carefully drafted to avoid ambiguity.

Define ownership clearly

Even in shared-care models, legal ownership must be identified.

Set out routine and responsibilities

If appropriate, agreements may include:

- feeding patterns,
- walking schedules,
- grooming,
- veterinary care arrangements,

- insurance contributions.

Include dispute resolution mechanisms

Agreements should specify how future disagreements will be addressed—through mediation, further arbitration or solicitor negotiation.

Use clear, concise language

Ambiguity can reignite disputes.

Handling High-Conflict or Coercive-Control Cases

7.23 NCDR may not be appropriate where:

- there is a history of coercive control;
- one party uses the pet as a form of control or intimidation;
- the animal's welfare is at risk;
- one party fears the other may harm the animal.

In such cases:

- safeguarding must be prioritised;
- non-molestation orders may be required;
- police or veterinary intervention may be needed;
- arbitration and mediation may be inappropriate.

Practitioners must exercise caution and assess risk carefully.

7.24 Given the limitations of the current statutory framework, NCDR is not merely an alternative; it is, in most cases, the *best* and most appropriate forum for resolving disputes involving beloved companion animals.

CHAPTER EIGHT

PET-NUPS

What is a Pet-Nup?

8.1 A Pet-Nup is an agreement between two people who own or intend to own a pet together. The purpose of the document is to set out how the owners will handle the care and ownership of their pet, together with any arrangements for the ongoing care and responsibilities meeting expenses, and what should happen to the pet should they decide to part ways. A Pet-Nup is a very important document to consider being drafted where there is a pet in a relationship, as it can help the parties have difficult conversations early on and prevent a lot of heartbreak and stress if the couple decide to separate later down the line.

8.2 A Pet-Nup, is very much like a nuptial agreement or cohabitation agreement and provisions for pets can be included in these types of documents. It can also be a standalone document.

8.3 The agreement will detail the living arrangements of the owner's pets in the event of a divorce or separation. At present, the only way in which to resolve a dispute regarding the arrangement of pets and their living situation is to make an application to the court or agree to NCDR. This can be costly for everyone involved but can be very emotive, with the added weight of an uncertain outcome. Pet-Nups provide couples with the option of working out and finalising the living situation of their pets, before disputes begin. It is a method of future-proofing the care of your pets, which in turn, ensures the best outcome for all involved.

8.4 As with any Nuptial agreement, a Pet-Nup should be prepared as a deed with a warning at the beginning that the owners intend for the agreement to be binding on both of them. it should also record that the owners have taken or have been told to take legal advice, and that they understand the terms of the deed and wish to be bound by it. It should also record that neither owner has been pressured into signing the agreement.

8.5 As set out in ***Radmacher v Granatino***[8] 'the court should give effect to a nuptial agreement that is freely entered into by each party with a full appreciation of its implications unless in the circumstances prevailing it would not be fair to hold the parties to their agreement'. In ***MN v AN***[2] the High Court confirmed that a pre-nuptial agreement would be upheld as there were no 'vitiating factors'. In most cases, if a nuptial agreement takes into account the criteria set out in ***Radmacher***, it will prevail.

8.6 That criteria from that case is as follows:

- There should be no undue pressure or coercion to enter into the agreement;
- Both parties should obtain independent legal advice to ensure that they have fully understood the terms of the agreement;
- The agreement should be fair;
- Full and frank should be provided, as deliberate non-disclosure would be treated as fraud/misrepresentation which is seen as a vitiating factor.

8 [2010] UKSC 42

Factors to consider in a Pet-Nup are:

1. Who will the pet live with? Will it live with one person alone and see the other person on certain days or will there be shared care – one week on, one week off?

2. If one owner is on holiday, will the pet stay with the other owner during this time or will they be looked after by someone else?

3. Who will care for the pet on a day-to-day basis?

4. How will you care for the pet? For example, will the pet mix with other animals, does the owner agree to provide a suitable environment for the pet, does the owner agree to protect the animal from pain and suffering?

5. Who will pay the vet bills?

6. Who will pay for the food and other expenses relating to the pet? Is it one person or both owners on a shared or unequal basis, if so, what are the %?

7. What diet will you pet have?

8. What are the owner's views on medical treatment and what do they agree the treatment their pet should receive in its lifetime?

8.7 It is also important to have conversations about ways in which you could provide the best life possible for your pet. The owners should consider which of them can provide their pet with more attention and care throughout the day. For example, if one person works full-time away from home, then this can be taken into account when looking at the arrangements regarding the pets and the best chance of providing quality time for their care.

8.8 As with Nuptial agreements, a Pet-Nup is not a legally enforceable document. Whilst they are not legally binding, they are being increasingly recognised and upheld if there are no vitiating factors. A Pet-Nup can make it easier for a judge to determine what will happen to the family pets if careful thought is applied and time has been spent in drafting such agreements.

CHAPTER NINE

COMPARATIVE AND INTERNATIONAL PERSPECTIVES

9.1 While English law continues to classify pets as property and applies traditional ownership principles in divorce disputes, many international jurisdictions have begun to modernise their approach. Over the past decade, several countries have recognised the special status of companion animals, elevating their treatment beyond the strict confines of chattel classification. These reforms, although varying in scope and depth, share a common recognition: pets are living beings with emotional bonds and welfare needs, not mere objects to be divided like furniture.

9.2 If we look at the international perspectives of how pets are treated on separation in law, we can see how far behind England and Wales are, as other countries are clearly taking welfare into account. The position is as follows:

- **Australia**: since 11 June 2024, pets are considered 'companion animals' – which is a particular form of property. The Family Law Act 1975 s.79(7) sets out factors to be considered such as, circumstances in which the animal was acquired, extent to which each party cared for the pet, any history of violence, attachment to the animal by a party or child and the law further provides that there shall be one single owner.

- **Canada (British Columbia)**: Amendments made to Canada's Family Law Act in 2024, introduced a special status to pets in financial proceedings. The law mandates that pets are 'companion animals' to be treated differently from other types of property.

9.3 This chapter examines key comparative models, exploring how different jurisdictions incorporate welfare, caregiving, and emotional attachment into their legal frameworks. It also analyses the strengths and limitations of these reforms and considers which elements might sensibly inform future developments in England and Wales. The goal of the Working Group on Pets on Divorce & Separation is not to argue for wholesale adoption of foreign systems, but to identify realistic, proportionate innovations compatible with English legal tradition and the realities of family justice.

The global movement towards animal welfare in family law

9.4 While no country treats pets exactly like children, nor would such a system be appropriate, an unmistakable legislative trend has emerged: courts are being granted a structured ability to consider the welfare of companion animals during family breakdown.

Several drivers underpin this trend:

- Growing public recognition of animal sentience;
- Increased social emphasis on mental health and emotional well-being;
- Demographic shifts toward smaller households and higher pet ownership;
- Greater understanding of animal behaviour and welfare science;
- Pressure from animal welfare organisations;
- Judicial frustration with outdated legal classifications.

These factors have prompted legislative and judicial developments that provide fertile ground for comparative analysis.

France

9.5 In 2015, the legislator created a new article 515-14 which now states: "*Animals are living beings with sensitivity. Subject to the laws that protect them, animals are subject to the regime of assets.*" This is significant progress, as pets were previously regarded as moveable assets.

In the event that a couple cannot decide the living arrangement of their pet on their separation, then the criteria used by the court take into account, is as follows:

1. The pet's well-being;
2. Ability to care for the pet;
3. Attachment to the pet;
4. Living conditions;
5. The presence of children.

9.6 In respect of reported cases, on 13 January 2011, Versailles Court of Appeal, no. 10/00572 handed down a ruling that awarded the dog to the husband on the grounds that '*the current living conditions [of the husband], who lives in a house with a garden, are more in line with the needs of this animal*'.

9.7 In a further ruling handed down on 29 January 2010, the Dijon Court of Appeal, no. 09/00941, considered that "*as the dog is of particular emotional importance to the two children, as revealed by their hearings and also by the psychological expertise, the first judge was right to award temporary right of us of the animal to the father with whom they live*".

9.8 All pets can potentially be considered as there does not seem to be any distinction in the law. It also depends upon whether the couple are married with or without a nuptial agreement (pre-nuptial or post-nuptial) or are unmarried.

9.9 If the separating couple are married without a nuptial agreement, then the default regime applies, which is a community regime. This means that any pet purchased or adopted before the marriage remains the property of the person who purchased or adopted it. If the pet was purchased or adopted after the parties married, then the pet becomes common property, despite who purchased or adopted it and should the couple not reach an agreement as to the future arrangements of their pet, then the court will decide.

9.10 If the separating couple have a nuptial agreement, then the ownership of the pet is determined by the terms of the contract. The person who adopts or purchases the pet will keep it after the divorce and it is also possible to take into account the registered named person on the 'Identification des Carnivores Domestique' (I-CAD) which is compulsory for cats, dogs and ferrets.

Spain

9.11 Spain undertook a significant reform in 2021 when it amended its Civil Code to recognise animals as sentient beings rather than property. This change was accompanied by a detailed statutory regime governing pet disputes in separation and divorce.

Spanish courts must now consider:

- the welfare and well-being of the animal;
- the emotional bond between each party and the pet;
- the animal's routines;
- risks of neglect or harm;

- the interests of children in the household;
- practical arrangements for ongoing care.

The court may order:

- sole care to one party;
- shared care;
- ongoing "visitation" arrangements;
- financial contributions for the pet's maintenance.

9.12 The reform aligns with Spain's broader civil law tradition, which already incorporates welfare principles in areas such as child arrangements and property rights. Spanish culture also places significant value on animal welfare, making the legislative shift both politically palatable and socially coherent.

9.13 The Spanish model requires court resources to monitor and enforce arrangements. Critics worry that introducing shared-care regimes may increase litigation. However, early commentary suggests most disputes remain privately resolved.

Portugal

9.14 Portugal followed a similar path, amending its Civil Code in 2017. The law now states that animals are sentient beings and that courts must consider their welfare in disputes arising from marital breakdown.

There was a change in the law which occurred through Law No. 8/2017, of March 3rd, establishing the legal status of animals for married couples, only. This law applies to all "companionship animals". However, this term does not have a legal definition. The only reference is to the criminal definition of a "companionship animal" implemented by Law No. 69/2014 which applies to “any animal kept or intended to be kept by humans, particularly in their home, for their entertainment and companionship”. As can be seen, this is a very broad definition of companion animals, which encompasses exotic animals, including birds, reptiles and small mammals.

When deciding on the future arrangements for the “companionship animal’s”, the court must consider the interests of each spouse, the interests if the spouse’s children, and the well-being of the companion animal.

Portuguese courts assess:

- which party can provide better conditions;
- the emotional and practical relationship between the animal and each party;
- whether one party poses a risk to the animal;
- the stability and predictability of each home environment.

Portugal explicitly permits shared-care orders where welfare considerations support them. This approach aims to reflect modern lifestyles and the reality that both parties may have bonded closely with the pet.

As with Spain, critics question whether courts should supervise shared-care arrangements, citing potential strain on judicial resources. Still, early judicial comments indicate the system is functioning without overwhelming the courts.

Germany

9.15 Germany amended its constitution (Grundgesetz) in 2002. The changes allowed animals to be recognised as beings with inherent dignity and rights. This elevated their legal status beyond that of mere property, which is how they were previously recognised. The amendment aligns with Germany's comprehensive Animal Welfare Act, which was adopted in 1998 and reflects a broader societal recognition of animal welfare.

The main points the court considers are as follows:

1) Who has been the primary carer;

2) Who can better meet the pet's needs; and

3) What arrangement best serves the pet's welfare.

Although in divorce proceedings, pets are considered part of the property settlement, since they are recognised as sentient beings, then their welfare is taken into account. With unmarried, pets are typically treated under general property law. The court will look at who legally owns the pet based on documentary evidence and who cares for and is responsible for the pet. In both scenarios, the pet's welfare plays a significant role in the court's decision making. Therefore, Spain reflects the broader approach of animal welfare law.

USA

9.15 Moving across the North Atlantic Ocean to California, since 2019, the court has been able to assign sole or joint ownership of a pet. Caselaw suggests that the main factors the court takes into account when deciding the care of the pet are: who the primary caregiver was during the marriage, the welfare of the pet, the history of the pet's care (including any evidence of neglect or abuse) and the emotional attachment of any children to the pet.

In New York, the first case dates back to 1999 in ***Raymond v Lachmann***[9], which was a case involving a dispute regarding a cat between roommates. The cat remained with the owner who had possession of it with Sheila Abdus-Salaam, J. stating: "*…we think it best for all concerned that, given his limited life expectancy, Lovey, who is now almost ten years old, remain where he has lived, prospered, loved and been loved for the past four years.*"

The state legislator amended the Domestic Relations Law on 25 October 2021, with a test similar to that of the determination of children's custody – the best interest analysis. This principal has been expanded and considered in recent caselaw, namely ***L.B. v. C.C. B.***[10], where it was stated:

> *"In determining the best interests of a companion animal under Domestic Relations Law § 236 (B) (5) (d) (15) the reviewing court should consider the totality of circumstances by weighing relevant factors applicable to the care of a companion animal. Salient factors for a court to consider include: the involvement, or absence, of each party in the companion animal's day-to-day life; the availability and willingness of each party to care for the companion animal; each party's involvement in health and veterinary care decisions; the quality of each party's respective home environment; the care and affection shown towards the companion animal; and each party's fitness and caretaking abilities. No single factor is dispositive."*

A "companion animal", under DRL §236(B)(5)(d)(15), shall have the same meaning as defined in the agriculture and markets law, which broadly means any dog, cat or domesticated animal normally maintained

9 [1999] 695 N.Y.S.2d 308 (N.Y. App. Div. 1999)

10 [2022] NYLJ LEXIS 1817

in or near the household of the owner or person who cares for such other domesticated animal but does not extend to "farm" animals.

Whilst the Domestic Relations Law only applies to married couples, unmarried couples are entitled to equitable distribution of a marital estate. However, they may also be able to argue that it would only be an equitable outcome to apply the a best-interest analysis to their companion animal(s), as well.

Canada: British Columbia

9.16 British Columbia introduced one of the most thoughtful and practical frameworks in the Western world through amendments to its Family Law Act in 2024.

The Act distinguishes between "companion animals" and other property. For companion animals, judges must consider:

- the extent of each party's care;
- the relationship between each party and the animal;
- the animal's needs;
- the risk of cruelty or family violence;
- any history of threats involving the animal;
- the suitability of living arrangements.

Importantly, the Act prohibits orders for shared ownership or property-style remedies where such arrangements would be contrary to the animal's welfare.

British Columbia's reforms strike a balance between:

- flexibility,
- welfare considerations,
- judicial discretion, and
- proportionality.

This model has been praised for being neither overly burdensome nor too vague. It is a model that The Working Group on Pets on Divorce & Separation favour.

British Columbia's approach provides a potential template for modest reform. Its emphasis on welfare, caregiving and safety could be adapted without importing an entire children-law framework.

New Zealand

9.17 Pets and animals are considered relationship property. Household pets are defined as 'family chattels' in The Property (Relationships) Act 1976 ("PRA"), Section 2. Despite when and how the household pet was acquired, they are considered relationship property pursuant to sections 8 (1)(b) and 10(4) of the PRA.

Section 2 the Act extensively defines that they are not limited to items of furniture or household amenities. Pets have the unique status of being the only living type of property classified as a "family chattel".

9.18 The courts have taken a more practical approach and what happens to the family chattels, is left to the discretion of the Judge, with their being a focus on considering the bond between pets and owners.

In ***Pence v Pence***[11], the court determined that it was in the best interests and welfare of the two chihuahuas to remain together.

In ***O'Brien v Tuer***[12], both parties sought the ownership of their pet dog. The respondent had the primary responsibility for the dog's day-to-day care when the parties were together. The applicant, without consulting the respondent, took the dog with her when she moved out of the family home. Ordering a settlement conference, the Court found that while pets are included in the definition of family chattels and ownership is addressed under the Act, the welfare of the dog was the primary consideration in determining the ownership.

9.20 In ***Sydney v Sydney***[13], one of the issues was who the parties' dog, Milo, should live with. The Court agreed with the principle in ***O'Brien v Tuer***[14], that the pet's welfare is the primary consideration when determining issues relating to custody. In ***Sydney***[15], Mrs Sydney sought a form of shared care of Milo and Mr Sydney disagreed, indicating that this would involve ongoing contact between the parties, which he did not want. The court also referred to ***C v D***[16], where it was determined that the party currently in possession of the dog does not have a stronger claim to the dog's long-term care than the other party.

In ***Sydney***[17], the dog had lived with Mr Sydney for the past two years and was attuned to an "outdoor lifestyle" and benefitted from the freedom of

---

[11] [1978] 2 MPC 146

[12] [District Court, Waitakere FP 090/327/03, 9 September 2003, Judge Mather]

[13] [2012] NZFC 2685

[14] (n 12)

[15] (n 13)

[16] [2011] NZFC 2685 (FC Auckland, 27 May 2011)

[17] (n 13)

its country lifestyle. At the time of the hearing Mrs Sydney was without permanent accommodation and it was likely that she would live in an urban setting, in the future.

The Judge favoured a "clean break" approach and decided that despite both parties being emotionally attached to Milo, that it was in Milo's best interests to continue living with Mr Sydney and for him to pay $425 to Mrs Sydney, which represented half of Milo's value.

9.21 In ***Wilkinson v Wilkinson***[18], the court was concerned about the care of Nelson (Maltese x Shih-Tzu) and Eric (Maltese). Both dogs had been in the long-term care of both parties and accepted that each party missed the dog who was in the care of the other owner. Mr Wilkinson wanted to retain Nelson with Mrs Wilkinson retaining Eric. Mrs Wilkinson wanted to retain both dogs. Taking into account the clean break approach but acknowledging the bond between the owners and their pets and the sadness the decision would bring to Mr Wilkinson, the Judge decided that Nelson was to remain with Mr Wilkinson and Eric was to remain with Mrs Wilkinson.

9.22 As can be seen, following the decision in ***Pence***[19], the Courts have generally treated disputes of family chattels, not unlike disputes regarding children, with the welfare and best interests of the animals being considered in determining who shall retain possession.

---

18 [2021] NZFC 8995

19 (n 11)

Australia

9.23 In **June 2025**, major reforms to Australia's family law framework came into effect under the *Family Law Amendment Act 2024 (Cth)*. These changes fundamentally change how courts deal with pets in the context of relationship breakdowns and property settlements.

For the first time, the *Family Law Act 1975* now recognises pets as "companion animals", a distinct category of property with its own statutory framework. This represents a departure from the historical approach where animals were treated no differently from inanimate chattels, with ownership determined primarily by title and contribution.

A companion animal is defined as an animal kept primarily for companionship, typically covering household pets such as dogs and cats. Certain animals are expressly excluded from this definition, for example, assistance animals under disability law, animals kept for business or agricultural purposes, and animals used in laboratory testing.

This change reflects a broader shift in legislative thinking: acknowledging that pets occupy a unique social and emotional role in family life and should be treated differently from other forms of property.

Under the amended Act (which commenced on 10 June 2025), when parties cannot agree on who keeps a companion animal following separation, the court may now make orders specifically in relation to the pet as part of property settlement proceedings.

The court's powers include:

- Granting sole ownership of a companion animal to one party;
- Transferring ownership to another person with consent; or
- Ordering sale of the companion animal.

9.24 Importantly, the legislation does not permit shared ownership or shared-care orders, the focus remains on allocating sole responsibility, mirroring the clean-break ethos in property and financial remedy proceedings.

When making decisions about companion animals, the court must consider a defined set of statutory factors rather than only title or financial contribution. These include:

- Attachment: whether a party or a child had a significant emotional bond with the animal;
- History of abuse or violence: including any family violence directed at the companion animal;
- Caregiving capacity: the ability of each party to provide for the animal's welfare in the future;
- Acquisition and ongoing care: how the pet was acquired and who primarily cared for it.

This list is designed to give courts clear guidance while avoiding open-ended welfare tests akin to those used for children. The reforms therefore introduce structured judicial discretion, rather than unfettered evaluative standards.

9.25 Alongside companion animal provisions, the June 2025 reforms also expand the way family violence is recognised in property proceedings. For the first time, the economic and broader effects of family violence, including where an abuser has harmed or threatened an animal are expressly included among the factors a court may consider when determining property settlements.

9.26 This is particularly significant for survivors of domestic abuse, as threats to pets are a well-documented form of coercive control. The new framework allows courts to take these dynamics into account when making ownership decisions, something that is especially valuable where an animal's safety and the survivor's welfare are intertwined.

9.27 The June 2025 amendments are part of a broader suite of changes to the *Family Law Act*'s property and financial provisions. These include providing the court with clearer statutory guidance on how property decisions should be approached generally, elevating duties of financial disclosure into the Act, and permitting the less adversarial approach to be applied more broadly in property proceedings.

9.28 While those broader reforms affect property settlement procedures overall, the changes specific to companion animals are distinct and significant because they acknowledge, for the first time in Australian federal law, that pets have a unique status in family breakdowns, both legally and practically.

9.29 Australia's June 2025 reforms are widely viewed as the most developed example of statutory recognition of pets in family law among common law jurisdictions. They do not create a welfare-driven regime similar to children's law, but they do provide a structured, forward-looking statutory approach that considers emotional bonds and caregiving in a way that previous law did not.

9.30 For family lawyers, these reforms offer a valuable model for thinking about how statutory guidance can bridge the gap between the law and the lived experience of separating families, which is something that England and Wales has not yet achieved.

9.31 For England and Wales, the lessons are clear: reform need not be radical to make a meaningful difference. Small, targeted legislative changes could align family law with modern societal values, reduce conflict, and provide courts with much-needed flexibility. This provides the backdrop for Chapter 9, which examines the work of the Working Group on Pets on Divorce & Separation and explores practical proposals for reform.

CHAPTER TEN

THE WORKING GROUP ON PETS ON DIVORCE & SEPARATION AND THE CASE FOR REFORM

10.1 The limitations of the current legal framework governing pets on divorce have prompted growing recognition within the family justice community that reform is necessary. As explored in previous chapters, the strict classification of pets as chattels fails to reflect modern family life, constrains judicial discretion, and often produces outcomes that feel emotionally or morally unsatisfactory for the parties involved. Against this backdrop, the Working Group on Pets on Divorce & Separation was established in 2025, bringing together leading figures across family law, veterinary welfare, behavioural science, and policy development.

10.2 This chapter examines the origins and structure of the Working Group, its aims, the research underpinning its proposals, and the reform pathways currently under consideration. It also reflects on the implications of reform for practitioners, courts, and clients, and considers how England and Wales might adopt a proportionate, welfare-informed approach without importing the complexity of a full children-law model.

Origins of the Working Group

10.3 The Working Group emerged from a shared recognition that existing law was unsatisfactory and ill-equipped to address modern pet-related disputes. Family practitioners repeatedly reported significant client distress when discovering that courts could not consider welfare or emotional bonds. Judges expressed frustration at the limits of their powers and the inadequacy of litigation for disputes involving beloved animals. Veterinary and behavioural experts highlighted the potential welfare implications of abrupt separation or inappropriate placements.

10.4 Pet ownership rose dramatically during and after the COVID-19 pandemic. As more couples acquired pets together, often as emotional support during lockdown, pet disputes grew in number and intensity. Many practitioners reported that pet issues were surfacing in many of their cases.

10.5 As jurisdictions such as Spain, Portugal, British Columbia and several US states adopted welfare-based frameworks, pressure grew within the UK for a modernised approach. The family law community recognised that England and Wales risked falling behind.

Composition of The Working Group

10.6 In response, the Working Group was formed, co-chaired by the author, Estella Newbold-Brown and Sarah Lucy Cooper. The Group comprises:

- family solicitors and barristers (including the authors);
- King's Counsel with expertise in financial remedies;
- veterinary surgeons;
- animal behaviourists;
- welfare organisations;
- actors and media personalities
- academics specialising in animal law;
- policy specialists;

- representatives from mediation and arbitration bodies.

The Working Group agreed early on that reform must be modest, proportionate and realistic, aligning with the principles of English family justice. The Group's approach is shaped by the following guiding principles:

Judicial discretion must remain central

10.7 Reform should not impose rigid solutions or encourage formulaic decision-making. Instead, the goal is to empower courts with a structured form of discretion that allows them to consider relevant welfare factors where appropriate.

Proportionality is essential

10.8 Any new legal framework must avoid burdening courts with extensive welfare hearings or expert evidence. Reform must not create a quasi–children law system for animals.

Emotional and welfare factors should be acknowledged

10.9 While pets should not be treated as children, the law should recognise that they form emotional bonds, have care needs, and experience distress. Allowing courts to take these factors into account creates more humane and credible outcomes.

Private agreements should remain primary

10.10 Reform should encourage parties to mediate or negotiate arrangements wherever possible. Litigation must remain the last resort.

The framework must be accessible and predictable

10.11 Statutory guidance should be clear, simple and easy to apply, guiding both litigants and practitioners.

Research undertaken by the Working Group

10.12 The Group reviewed legislative reforms in several jurisdictions across the globe. Particular attention was paid to the balance between welfare considerations and proportionality.

Solicitors, barristers and mediators provided qualitative data on:

- frequency of pet disputes;
- common points of conflict;
- drafting challenges;
- typical client expectations;
- emotional impact on parties;
- the effectiveness of mediation and arbitration.

Veterinary professionals provided evidence on:

- the behavioural impact of abrupt separation;
- the importance of routine;
- stress indicators in dogs and cats;
- the risks posed by unsuitable living arrangements;

- the welfare consequences of forced separation of bonded animals.

Judges contributed commentary on:

- current limitations of legal powers;
- proportionality concerns;
- concerns about increased litigation;
- the need for clarity and structured discretion.

10.13 The Working Group identified several core problems:

Lack of welfare consideration

Courts cannot consider welfare even where ownership is ambiguous or where an animal's wellbeing may be at risk.

Harsh outcomes where ownership does not reflect care

Clients who served as primary caregivers often lose pets because documentation suggests the other party is the legal owner.

No power to order transitional arrangements

Courts cannot order phased handovers, which can harm both animals and owners.

No power to order shared arrangements

Even where parties agree shared care is appropriate, courts cannot impose it.

Inconsistent private agreements

Lack of legal structure leads to unpredictable and sometimes unenforceable informal arrangements.

Emotional distress and increased conflict

The rigid legal framework often escalates disputes, harming both parties and sometimes the pet.

The Working Group's preferred model

10.14 After extensive consultation and analysis, the Working Group identified a preferred framework comprising four components:

1. A statutory welfare checklist for pet disputes

This limited checklist would include:

- caregiving history;
- the emotional bond between each party and the animal;
- the animal's routine and stability;
- suitability of living arrangements;
- risk of harm, neglect or coercive control;
- the interests of children.

This would not replicate the Children Act welfare test but would provide humane and proportionate guidance.

2. Judicial power to order transitional arrangements

A phased handover could significantly reduce distress for both pets and parties.

3. Judicial discretion to order shared arrangements where appropriate

Shared care would remain exceptional but possible.

4. Strong emphasis on NCDR

Legislation and FPR guidance would direct parties toward mediation or arbitration before litigation.

This model balances welfare, practicality and proportionality.

Implications for practitioners

10.15 Reform would reshape practice in several ways:

- advice on welfare factors would become essential;
- evidence-gathering would expand to include caregiving history;
- creative drafting of transitional arrangements would be normalised;
- practitioners would take a more active role in guiding clients into NCDR;
- pet disputes could become more predictable and less adversarial.

The future of pet disputes in family law

10.16 The Working Group anticipates that pet disputes will continue to rise. Families increasingly view animals as members of the household, and welfare science continues to evolve. Public support for reform is strong, and comparative models demonstrate that modernisation is both practical and beneficial.

10.17 Reform in England and Wales is not about equating pets with children, nor about creating complex litigation. It is about recognising reality: pets are sentient beings with emotional bonds and welfare needs, and courts require tools to respond humanely and proportionately.

10.18 The Working Group represents a landmark shift in how family justice understands and responds to disputes involving companion animals. Its interdisciplinary, evidence-based approach offers a credible, proportionate framework for reform, one that aligns with societal expectations, international developments, and the welfare needs of pets, while safeguarding judicial resources and preserving proportionality.

10.19 Reform is not only possible but necessary. Modern family life demands a legal system that acknowledges the role pets play in our emotional landscapes. England and Wales now stand at a crossroads: the current structure is increasingly out of step with reality, but with targeted reform, the law can evolve to meet the needs of families and the animals they love.

10.20 The Working Group on Pets in Divorce and Separation were highly commended in the Community interaction Award at the Family Law Awards 2025.

CHAPTER ELEVEN

POTENTIAL REFORM TO THE LAW IN ENGLAND AND WALES

11.1 The treatment of pets on divorce in England and Wales is increasingly difficult to justify. It is the author's view that the current legal framework is poorly aligned with modern family life, social expectations, and the realities faced daily by family law practitioners. Companion animals now occupy a central role in many households, providing emotional support, structure and continuity. Yet on separation, the law continues to treat pets as chattels, to be allocated according to orthodox principles of ownership, with little scope for nuance or welfare-based reasoning.11.2 This chapter considers that reform is now both necessary and achievable. It does not propose a wholesale reimagining of family law or the importation of child-law concepts into pet disputes. Rather, it advances the case for a proportionate, structured reform based on the Australian model, which recognises pets as a distinct category of property while preserving finality, certainty and procedural restraint.

11.3 As explored in earlier chapters, the English courts' approach to pets is constrained by statute and long-standing property principles. Pets fall within the ambit of section 24 of the Matrimonial Causes Act 1973 and are treated no differently from other chattels. Ownership, rather than caregiving, attachment or welfare, remains the decisive consideration. Shared-care arrangements are almost never ordered, and courts are reluctant to craft outcomes that require ongoing cooperation between former partners.

11.4 While judges often acknowledge the emotional importance of pets, case law demonstrates consistent judicial reluctance to move beyond a narrow ownership analysis. This is not a failure of judicial imagination, but a reflection of statutory constraint. The result is a system in which outcomes may be legally correct but emotionally unsatisfactory, and in which clients frequently feel that the law has failed to engage with the substance of their dispute.

11.5 From a practitioner's perspective, these limitations generate predictable difficulties. Pet disputes can derail negotiations, inflame conflict, and consume disproportionate time and resources. The court's inability to consider welfare or routine means that many disputes are better resolved outside litigation, placing increasing pressure on practitioners to steer clients towards non-court dispute resolution. While mediation and arbitration offer valuable alternatives, reliance on these mechanisms alone cannot fully compensate for the absence of a clear statutory framework.

11.6 Internationally, England and Wales are increasingly out of step. A number of jurisdictions have reformed their approach to pets on separation, recognising that companion animals occupy a position distinct from inanimate property. Among these, Australia offers the most instructive model for reform within a common law system comparable to England and Wales.

Australia

11.7 Australia's legislative trajectory culminated in amendments to the *Family Law Act 1975* that came into force in June 2024. Under the amended provisions, pets are treated as "companion animals", a specific category of property subject to tailored statutory guidance. Crucially, pets remain part of the property regime; they are not elevated to the status of children, nor are courts invited to conduct open-ended welfare inquiries. Instead, the legislation directs the court to consider a defined list of factors when determining ownership of a companion animal on separation. These include the circumstances in which the animal was acquired, the extent to which each party cared for it, any history of family violence or animal abuse, the attachment of a party or child to the animal, and each party's capacity to meet the animal's ongoing needs. The court is required to allocate ownership to one party only, thereby avoiding shared-care arrangements and preserving finality.

11.8 This approach strikes a careful balance. It acknowledges that pets are not interchangeable with other forms of property, while resisting the creation of a parallel welfare jurisdiction. It provides structured discretion rather than unfettered judicial choice, reducing uncertainty and limiting the scope for disproportionate litigation.

11.9 The strength of the Australian model lies in its restraint. It recognises emotional reality without allowing emotion to dominate legal analysis. By confining the court's task to a single ownership decision, it avoids the enforcement difficulties and ongoing conflict associated with shared-care arrangements. At the same time, it allows courts to reach outcomes that better reflect lived experience, particularly where ownership documentation is ambiguous or where caregiving has been clearly one-sided.

11.10 Importantly, there is no evidence that the Australian reforms have led to an explosion of litigation or unmanageable judicial workloads. On the contrary, the clarity provided by statutory factors appears to assist resolution, whether through negotiated settlement or judicial determination. For practitioners, the model offers predictability and a clearer framework within which to advise clients.

11.11 Adopting a similar approach in England and Wales would require modest legislative amendment rather than wholesale reform. Pets could be defined statutorily as a distinct category of property within the Matrimonial Causes Act 1973 or related legislation, with courts directed to consider a limited set of factors when determining ownership. The clean break principle would remain intact, and the court's powers would continue to be exercised within financial remedy proceedings.

11.12 Such reform would bring several advantages. It would align family law more closely with societal expectations and with wider legal recognition of animal sentience. It would reduce the sense of injustice experienced by primary carers whose contributions currently carry little legal weight. It would also support earlier and more constructive resolution of disputes, as parties would have a clearer understanding of the factors likely to influence outcomes.

11.13 From a practitioner's standpoint, a statutory framework of this kind would enhance, rather than undermine, existing best practice. It would sit alongside non-court dispute resolution, not replace it, providing a principled backdrop against which mediation and arbitration could operate. It would also relieve some of the burden currently placed on practitioners to bridge the gap between law and lived experience through negotiation alone.

11.14 The case for reform should not be overstated. The Australian model does not transform pets into quasi-children, nor does it invite courts to engage in subjective assessments of an animal's "best interests" in the abstract. It represents an incremental evolution, grounded in practicality and informed by experience.

11.15 As pressures on the family justice system continue to mount, and as pet ownership becomes ever more embedded in family life, the question is no longer whether the current framework is imperfect, but how long it can remain unchanged. The Australian model offers a clear, workable answer. It provides a template for reform that is principled, proportionate and compatible with the realities of practice in England and Wales.

CHAPTER TWELVE

WHAT DOES ALL OF THIS MEAN FOR FAMILY PRACTITIONERS?

12.1 The growing prominence of pets in family law disputes is not a passing trend. It reflects deeper changes in how families are formed, how emotional bonds are experienced, and how loss is felt on separation. For family law practitioners, disputes about pets have become a recurring and often difficult feature of practice. This chapter draws together the themes explored throughout this book and considers what they mean in practical terms for those advising separating families.

12.2 One of the clearest messages to emerge is that pet disputes require a different approach from other financial issues. Although pets are treated as chattels in law, they do not function as ordinary property in practice. Clients rarely experience disputes about pets as financial questions. Instead, they are bound up with grief, identity and the fear of further loss. For practitioners, this means recognising early on that standard financial remedy approaches may not translate effectively. A client who is willing to compromise on pension sharing or property division may take an inflexible stance when it comes to a dog or cat.

12.3 Expectation management emerges as one of the most important skills in this area. Many clients approach pet disputes with assumptions that do not reflect the legal framework: that the court will prioritise welfare, that caregiving will outweigh ownership, or that shared care can be ordered. Correcting these assumptions is essential, but how this is done matters.

12.4 Pet disputes highlight the importance of proportionality in family proceedings. While emotionally significant, they are often financially modest. Allowing such disputes to dominate litigation can lead to disproportionate costs, delay and entrenchment. Practitioners therefore need to make conscious strategic decisions about how and when pet disputes are addressed. Early identification, focused evidence-gathering and clear advice about likely outcomes can prevent escalation. In some cases, resolving the pet issue early may unlock progress on wider financial matters; in others, it may be more effective to address it alongside settlement discussions. Either way, leaving pet disputes to the margins of a case rarely produces good outcomes.

NCDR

12.5 This book has repeatedly returned to the limitations of the court's powers in pet disputes. For practitioners, the practical consequence is clear: non-court dispute resolution is not simply an option but often the most appropriate forum for resolution.

12.6 Mediation and arbitration allow space for welfare, routine and emotional attachment to be considered openly, without the constraints imposed by statute. They enable creative solutions that the court cannot impose and can preserve a degree of goodwill where ongoing contact is unavoidable.

12.7 Practitioners play a crucial role in framing these processes positively. Presenting NCDR as a pragmatic choice rather than a compromise can help clients engage constructively and avoid the disappointment that often follows litigation.

Drafting and precision

12.8 Where agreement is reached, drafting assumes particular importance. Ambiguous or informal arrangements can lead to future disputes, especially where emotions remain raw. Practitioners should ensure that ownership is clearly addressed in any consent order and that responsibility for registration, insurance and veterinary care is unambiguous.

12.9 At the same time, practitioners must be clear with clients about the enforceability of any welfare-based or shared arrangements. Recording such arrangements outside the operative order may be appropriate, but only with proper advice about their legal status.

Ethical and safeguarding considerations

12.10 Pet disputes can raise ethical and safeguarding issues, particularly in high-conflict cases or where there is a history of coercive control. Pets may be used as a means of exerting pressure, maintaining contact or inflicting emotional harm. Threats relating to pets can form part of a wider pattern of abusive behaviour.

12.11 Practitioners must remain alert to these dynamics and avoid inadvertently facilitating them. In some cases, encouraging shared arrangements or informal agreements may expose a client or an animal to risk. Professional judgment and safeguarding awareness are therefore essential.

Looking ahead

12.12 The increasing visibility of pet disputes reflects broader shifts in family life and in public expectations of the justice system. Whether or not reform is imminent, practitioners can expect these disputes to become more common, not less.

CHAPTER THIRTEEN

CONCLUSION

13.1 Disputes about pets on separation expose a fault line in modern family law. On the one hand, companion animals are embedded in family life in ways that are emotionally significant, practically complex, and often central to a client's sense of stability and wellbeing. On the other hand, English law continues to approach pets through the narrow lens of property, applying law developed for inanimate chattels to living, sentient beings. The result is a body of law that is increasingly disconnected from lived reality.

13.2 Throughout this book, a consistent picture emerges. The court's approach to pet disputes is constrained, ownership-driven and pragmatic. Judges are sympathetic but limited. Case law repeatedly confirms that emotional attachment, caregiving and welfare cannot displace legal ownership, and that shared-care arrangements will almost never be imposed. Property adjustment orders offer clarity but little nuance. Where disputes escalate, outcomes can feel arbitrary or unjust, not because judges err in law, but because the law itself is ill-equipped to deal with the problem it is asked to solve. These themes run through the authorities and are reflected in everyday practice

13.3 For practitioners, the consequences are practical and immediate. Pet disputes frequently become the most emotionally charged aspect of a case, even where their financial value is modest. They can derail negotiations, inflame conflict, and undermine otherwise sensible settlement discussions. Managing these disputes therefore requires not only technical legal knowledge, but judgment, empathy and insight. Early expectation management, careful evidence-gathering, precise drafting and a firm grasp of the court's limitations are essential tools. So too is a willingness to guide clients away from litigation where the court cannot deliver the outcome they seek.

13.4 Non-court dispute resolution emerges as a central theme for good reason. Mediation, arbitration and collaborative processes offer the flexibility that the statutory framework lacks. They allow space for welfare-based discussion, for recognition of emotional bonds, and for creative solutions that prioritise stability for both the animal and the parties. In many cases, these processes are not merely preferable but necessary if humane and durable outcomes are to be achieved. The increasing judicial emphasis on NCDR reinforces this reality and places a corresponding responsibility on practitioners to engage with these options proactively.

13.5 Looking beyond England and Wales, comparative models demonstrate that the current position is not inevitable. Other jurisdictions have shown that it is possible to recognise the unique status of companion animals without importing a child-law framework or undermining finality in financial proceedings. The Australian model, in particular, offers a compelling example of proportionate reform: pets remain part of the property regime, but courts are given structured guidance to consider caregiving, attachment and welfare, while still requiring allocation to a single owner. This approach aligns legal outcomes more closely with social reality, without creating open-ended or unmanageable obligations.

13.6 Whether and when reform will be enacted in England and Wales remains uncertain. What is clear, however, is that the existing framework places an increasing burden on practitioners to bridge the gap between law and lived experience. Until statutory change occurs, family lawyers will continue to play a pivotal role in shaping outcomes through advice, negotiation and creative problem-solving. The challenge is to work within the constraints of the law while minimising harm, managing expectations honestly, and helping clients navigate some of the most emotionally difficult decisions they will face on separation.

13.7 This book has sought to provide a practical guide to that task: to explain the law as it stands, to analyse how it is applied in practice, to explore alternative routes to resolution, and to situate English law within a broader international context. Above all, it aims to equip family lawyers with the tools to handle pet disputes with clarity, confidence and sensitivity, recognising that while pets may be treated as property in law, they are rarely experienced that way by the families who love them.

'The Electronic Communications Code: A Practical Guide – Second Edition' by Kerry Bretherton KC, James Castle, Mark Loveday
'A Practical Guide to the Independent School Standards – September 2023 Edition' by Sarah McKimm
'A Practical Guide to Estate Administration and Crypto Assets' by Richard Marshall
'A Practical Guide to Parental Alienation in Private and Public Law Children Cases' by Sam King QC & Frankie Shama
'Contested Heritage – Removing Art from Land and Historic Buildings' by Richard Harwood QC, Catherine Dobson, David Sawtell
'The Limits of Separate Legal Personality: When Those Running a Company Can Be Held Personally Liable for Losses Caused to Third Parties Outside of the Company' by Dr Mike Wilkinson
'A Practical Guide to Transgender Law' by Robin Moira White & Nicola Newbegin
'A Practical Guide to 'Stranded Spouses' in Family Law' by Mani Singh Basi
'A Practical Guide to Residential Freehold Conveyancing' by Lorraine Richardson
'A Practical Guide to Pensions on Divorce for Lawyers' by Bryan Scant
'A Practical Guide to Challenging Sham Marriage Allegations in Immigration Law' by Priya Solanki
'A Practical Guide to Digital Communications Evidence in Criminal Law' by Sam Willis
'A Practical Guide to Legal Rights in Scotland' by Sarah-Jane Macdonald
'A Practical Guide to New Build Conveyancing' by Paul Sams & Rebecca East
'A Practical Guide to Inherited Wealth on Divorce' by Hayley Trim
'A Practical Guide to Practice Direction 12J and Domestic Abuse in Private Law Children Proceedings' by Rebecca Cross & Malvika Jaganmohan
'A Practical Guide to Confiscation and Restraint' by Narita Bahra QC, John Carl Townsend, David Winch
'A Practical Guide to the Law of Forests in Scotland' by Philip Buchan
'A Practical Guide to Health and Medical Cases in Immigration Law' by Rebecca Chapman & Miranda Butler
'A Practical Guide to Bad Character Evidence for Criminal Practitioners by Aparna Rao
'A Practical Guide to Extradition Law post-Brexit' by Myles Grandison et al
'A Practical Guide to Hoarding and Mental Health for Housing Lawyers' by Rachel Coyle

'Stephens on Contractual Indemnities' by Richard Stephens
'A Practical Guide to the EU Succession Regulation' by Richard Frimston
'A Practical Guide to Solicitor and Client Costs – Second Edition' by Robin Dunne
'Constructive Dismissal – Practice Pointers and Principles' by Benjimin Burgher
'A Practical Guide to Religion and Belief Discrimination Claims in the Workplace' by Kashif Ali
'A Practical Guide to the Law of Medical Treatment Decisions' by Ben Troke
'Fundamental Dishonesty and QOCS in Personal Injury Proceedings: Law and Practice' by Jake Rowley
'A Practical Guide to the Law in Relation to School Exclusions' by Charlotte Hadfield & Alice de Coverley
'A Practical Guide to Divorce for the Silver Separators' by Karin Walker
'The Right to be Forgotten – The Law and Practical Issues' by Melissa Stock
'A Practical Guide to Planning Law and Rights of Way in National Parks, the Broads and AONBs' by James Maurici QC, James Neill et al
'A Practical Guide to Election Law' by Tom Tabori
'A Practical Guide to the Law in Relation to Surrogacy' by Andrew Powell
'A Practical Guide to Claims Arising from Fatal Accidents – Second Edition' by James Patience
'A Practical Guide to Asbestos Claims' by Jonathan Owen & Gareth McAloon
'A Practical Guide to Stamp Duty Land Tax in England and Northern Ireland' by Suzanne O'Hara
'A Practical Guide to the Law of Farming Partnerships' by Philip Whitcomb
'A Practical Guide to the Law of Unlawful Eviction and Harassment – Second Edition' by Stephanie Lovegrove
'A Practical Guide to Costs in Personal Injury Claims – Second Edition' by Matthew Hoe
'A Practical Guide to the General Data Protection Regulation (GDPR) – Second Edition' by Keith Markham
'A Practical Guide to Working with Litigants in Person and McKenzie Friends in Family Cases' by Stuart Barlow
'Protecting Unregistered Brands: A Practical Guide to the Law of Passing Off' by Lorna Brazell
'A Practical Guide to Secondary Liability and Joint Enterprise Post-Jogee' by Joanne Cecil & James Mehigan

'A Practical Guide to the Pre-Action RTA Claims Protocol for Personal Injury Lawyers' by Antonia Ford
'A Practical Guide to Neighbour Disputes and the Law' by Alexander Walsh
'A Practical Guide to Coercive Control for Legal Practitioners and Victims' by Rachel Horman
'A Practical Guide to the Law of Driverless Cars – Second Edition'
by Alex Glassbrook, Emma Northey & Scarlett Milligan
'A Practical Guide to TOLATA Claims' by Greg Williams
'A Practical Guide to Elderly Law – Second Edition' by Justin Patten
'A Practical Guide to Responding to Housing Disrepair and Unfitness Claims' by Iain Wightwick
'A Practical Guide to the Law of Bullying and Harassment in the Workplace' by Philip Hyland
'How to Be a Freelance Solicitor: A Practical Guide to the SRA-Regulated Freelance Solicitor Model' by Paul Bennett
'A Practical Guide to Prison Injury Claims' by Malcolm Johnson
'A Practical Guide to Advising Clients at the Police Station' by Colin Stephen McKeown-Beaumont
'A Practical Guide to Antisocial Behaviour Injunctions – Second Edition' by Iain Wightwick
'Practical Mediation: A Guide for Mediators, Advocates, Advisers, Lawyers, and Students in Civil, Commercial, Business, Property, Workplace, and Employment Cases' by Jonathan Dingle with John Sephton
'The Mini-Pupillage Workbook' by David Boyle
'A Practical Guide to Crofting Law' by Brian Inkster
'A Practical Guide to the Law of Domain Names and Cybersquatting' by Andrew Clemson
'A Practical Guide to the Law of Gender Pay Gap Reporting' by Harini Iyengar
'NHS Whistleblowing and the Law' by Joseph England
'Employment Law and the Gig Economy' by Nigel Mackay & Annie Powell
'A Practical Guide to Noise Induced Hearing Loss (NIHL) Claims' by Andrew Mckie, Ian Skeate, Gareth McAloon
'An Introduction to Beauty Negligence Claims – A Practical Guide for the Personal Injury Practitioner' by Greg Almond
'Intercompany Agreements for Transfer Pricing Compliance' by Paul Sutton
'Zen and the Art of Mediation' by Martin Plowman
'A Practical Guide to Adoption for Family Lawyers' by Graham Pegg

'A Practical Guide to Industrial Disease Claims' by Andrew Mckie & Ian Skeate
'A Practical Guide to Conducting a Sheriff Court Proof' by Andrew Stevenson
'A Practical Guide to Vicarious Liability' by Mariel Irvine
'A Practical Guide to Applications for Landlord's Consent and Variation of Leases' by Mark Shelton
'A Practical Guide to Relief from Sanctions Post-Mitchell and Denton' by Peter Causton
'A Practical Guide to Equity Release for Advisors' by Paul Sams
'A Practical Guide to Financial Services Claims' by Chris Hegarty
'A Practical Guide to Financial Ombudsman Service Claims' by Adam Temple & Robert Scrivenor
'A Practical Guide to Running Housing Disrepair and Cavity Wall Claims – Second Edition' by Andrew Mckie & Ian Skeate
'A Practical Guide to Holiday Sickness Claims – Second Edition' by Andrew Mckie & Ian Skeate
'Arguments and Tactics for Personal Injury and Clinical Negligence Claims' by Dorian Williams
'A Practical Guide to Drone Law' by Rufus Ballaster, Andrew Firman, Eleanor Clot
'On Experts: CPR35 for Lawyers and Experts' by David Boyle
'An Introduction to Personal Injury Law' by David Boyle

These books and more are available to order online direct from the publisher at www.lawbriefpublishing.com, where you can also read free sample chapters. For any queries, call us on 0844 587 2383 or email us at mail@lawbriefpublishing.com.

Our books are all generally in stock at www.amazon.co.uk with free next day delivery for Prime members, and at good legal bookshops such as Wildy & Sons.

We are regularly launching new books in our series of practical day-to-day practitioners' guides. Visit our website and join our free newsletter to be kept informed and to receive special offers, free chapters, etc.

You can also follow us on Twitter at www.twitter.com/lawbriefpub.

www.ingramcontent.com/pod-product-compliance
Ingram Content Group UK Ltd.
Pitfield, Milton Keynes, MK11 3LW, UK
UKHW020148290926
15471UKWH00004B/759

9 781918 241280